PROBLEMS IN THE THEORY OF KNOWLEDGE

PROBLÈMES DE LA THÉORIE DE LA CONNAISSANCE

INTERNATIONAL INSTITUTE OF PHILOSOPHY
ENTRETIENS IN HELSINKI
24–27 August 1970

PROBLEMS
IN THE THEORY OF
KNOWLEDGE

edited by

G. H. VON WRIGHT

MARTINUS NIJHOFF / THE HAGUE / 1972

INSTITUT INTERNATIONAL DE PHILOSOPHIE

ENTRETIENS DE HELSINKI

24–27 août 1970

PROBLÈMES DE LA THÉORIE DE LA CONNAISSANCE

édités par les soins de

G. H. VON WRIGHT

MARTINUS NIJHOFF / LA HAYE / 1972

ISBN 90 247 1203 3

TABLE DES MATIÈRES

PREFACE

At its meeting at Heidelberg in September 1969 the Institut International de Philosophie decided to hold its next *Entretiens* in Helsinki. The theme selected for the meeting in Finland was Problems in the Theory of Knowledge (*Problèmes de la théorie de la connaissance*).

The Entretiens de Helsinki took place from 24th to 27th August 1970. As local host organization, the Philosophical Society of Finland was responsible for the external and social arrangements of the Entretiens. A grant from the Finnish Ministry of Education and the Oskar Öflund Foundation had been obtained for the purpose. 40 members of the Institut participated in the Entretiens. The various sessions, which were also open to members of the Philosophical Society of Finland, were attended by on average 100 people.

The scholarly programme had been planned jointly by Sir Alfred Ayer, President of the I.I.P., and by Professor G. H. von Wright, President of the P.S.F. It was originally designed to consist of four sections devoted to the special topics of perception, memory, evidence, and the definition of knowledge. Efforts to find speakers on the first topic failed, and it was decided to devote one section of the Entretiens to Wittgenstein's theory of knowledge.

For every section a main speaker (*rapporteur*) and commentator (*interlocuteur*) were selected. In the section on the definition of knowledge Professor Bernard Williams (Cambridge) was main speaker and Sir Alfred Ayer (Oxford) commentator, in the section on evidence Professor André Mercier (Bern) and Professor Paul Ricoeur (Paris), and in the section on Wittgenstein Professor G. H. von Wright (Helsinki) and Mr. Brian McGuinness (Oxford). In the section on memory, finally, independent papers were presented by Professor Edmund Furlong (Dublin) and Professor Eduardo Nicol (Mexico City) At the concluding session of the Entretiens a summary of the papers and discussion was presented by Professor Ch. Perelman (Brussels).

Preface

The papers and replies, with the exception of Professor Ricoeur's, are here printed in final and in most cases somewhat expanded versions, especially prepared by the authors for this volume. The discussions were not recorded and no efforts have been made to summarize them for publication. An appendix to the volume is a paper "Kant et la connaissance de soi" by J. N. Théodoracopoulos, Secretary General of the Academy of Athens.

B. A. O. WILLIAMS

(*University of Cambridge*)

KNOWLEDGE AND REASONS

One aim of this paper is to make some suggestions about the role of reasons in knowledge. The other is to sketch an approach to the nature of knowledge which will put that question into a correct perspective. That sketch will indeed be sketchy, and most of what I shall say schematic. My aim is to put the main issues into what seems to me the right overall shape.

1. *Propositional and practical knowledge*

I shall be concerned only with what I shall call *propositional* knowledge, knowledge whose paradigmatic expression in language-users is the confident assertion of truths, and where the claim that it is knowledge that is being expressed involves as a necessary condition that what is asserted is true. This contrasts with *practical* knowledge, of which the paradigmatic expression is the skilful and successful performance of some task. (Success is not, however, related to practical knowledge as truth is to propositional knowledge: without truth of the proposition there is no propositional knowledge, but practical knowledge can be present and in action, though robbed of success through extrinsic causes.)

The distinction is not easy to formulate, and admits borderline cases. It is, however, both genuine and ineliminable, neither sort of knowledge being reducible to the other; this I shall assume here without argument. I shall make two further remarks about the distinction, both relevant to what follows. First, I use the term *propositional*, and not the term hallowed by history for this contrast, *theoretical*, because the latter too readily imports the notion of the systematic. Some propositional knowledge is indeed theoretical, in the sense of being general, systematically arranged, having a structure of laws, etc.; but much propositional knowledge is not. The idea that what contrasts with practice is in *that* sense theory, can generate serious confusion (present, I think, in the reflections of

Michael Oakeshott in his *Rationalism in Politics* and elsewhere). Second, I do not think that the distinction is very happily labelled, as by Ryle, as a distinction between *knowing that* and *knowing how*. These labels are of course all right if merely labels. But their use can encourage the neglect of several facts, some of them important. For example, not every ascription of propositional knowledge need, or even can, take as it stands the form "A knows that...." "Know" importantly governs indirect questions (as in, notably, "A knows whether..."). The philosophical relevance of this fact will come up in (2) below. On the other hand "A knows how..." can represent propositional knowledge ("A knows how a nuclear power station works"); what represents practical knowledge is rather "A knows how to...." But then there is no peculiarity with "how": practical knowledge can equally be represented by "A knows when to..., what to..." etc. Following from that, some cases of "A knows that ..." can represent practical knowledge, if they further involve "to" (or equivalent construction) and (something like) a demonstrative: "A knows that this is the time to add the salt," "A knows that the one to use is the one that looks like this" etc.

I should perhaps add that I do not regard peculiar properties of the English language as very illuminating for the concept of knowledge; but they can serve to remind one of the misleading possibilities of labels themselves drawn from that language.

2. "Knowing that" and the examiner's situation

Philosophers who have addressed themselves to the third-personal issue (and have not, like Descartes, concentrated on "What do I know?" – a concentration which raises its own problems) have tended to stick to the question of the truth-conditions of "A knows that p." That is to say, they have looked for conditions sufficient for giving an affirmative answer to the question "does A know that p?". In actual life, one very natural implication of asking that question is that the speaker himself knows that p, and is asking whether A does. One immediate effect of taking as central that question, which has that implication, is to push into the background an important class of cases: the cases, namely, where the speaker does not know how things stand with regard to p, and wants to find someone who does – a situation in which he could ask "who knows whether p?" or "does A know whether p?". We have already a concentration which helps us to forget a banal and important fact: knowers are, for others, sources of information.

Even in sticking to "A knows that p," however, the concentration tends to go in one only of several possible directions. The one favoured is that in which the point of the question is whether A's cognitive relation to the truth that p is adequate: in particular, the case where A is admittedly convinced of the truth that p, and the question is whether that conviction is adequately based. This situation, and more generally the situation in which informed questioners are concerned with A's credentials with regard to a piece of knowledge, we might call the *examiner's situation*. It is far from typical in practice. For instance, another and frequent situation with respect to the question "does A know that p?" is that in which the point of the question is to ask whether the information that p has *got out* to A, or *got round* to him: one of our interests in knowledge is where it has got to. Where such is our interest, the stress on credentials (the relevance of which to the examiner's situation is self-explanatory) is less to the fore. When my interest is whether A has come to know something which, for instance, it would be better for me if he did not know, the central question is whether the information has got to him, and he believes it, and less whether the reasons with which A would support his belief are strong or adequate reasons. Yet even in such a case, there is a contrast with A's merely having come to believe the proposition in question, a contrast embedded in the thought that the information has "got to" him. If he has come to know, then at least it is the case that he has not merely guessed – there must be a route by which the information has come to him, and the fact that what he believes is true must have contributed in some appropriate way to his having come to believe it. In this last consideration, obscure though it is, we shall see a central condition on the concept of knowledge.

Let us return to the cases in which our interest in another's possession of knowledge concerns a matter about which we lack knowledge: our concern (unlike the examiner's) is to find out, not so much about this person, as about the matter in hand. If "p" represents some sentence which may be used to make a statement of fact, let "wh-p" represent in general direct and (with any necessary grammatical modification) indirect questions that may be formed out of that sentence. The simplest example of an indirect question, available in every case, is "whether p." But there are of course many other and various possibilities; if "p" mentions some time ("the train leaves at 15.00 hrs") "wh-p" can be a "when"-question ("when does the train leave?" "...when the train leaves"); if "p" mentions a place, "wh-p" can be a "where"-question, etc. Now the following statements all seem to me to be true:

a. In many standard situations, all that is necessary for it to be the case that A knows wh-p – besides his actually being right in this case (see (b) below) – are such things as that A is almost always right about matters of this kind, because e.g., in the matter of the train, he has learned up the time-table; or that we know, what perhaps A himself does not know, that A has come by his beliefs on this subject by reliable means. Thus it may be that A has come by his beliefs from having been told by B, and we know that B is a reliable authority on these matters, though A himself may not, never (for instance) having reflected on that question.

b. If conditions of this kind are satisfied, then all that is further necessary for it to be the case that A knows wh-p is that the beliefs he has with regard to the question be true, i.e. that he actually be right. (I shall assume throughout this paper that *belief*, involving a fair degree of conviction, is a necessary condition of knowledge. I doubt whether that is true without qualification, but the assumption will serve for the present discussion.)

c. If A knows wh-p, and P is the class of correct answers to the question "wh-p?," then for some member of P, q, A knows that q. This rather cumbrous formulation is intended to allow for such facts as that if "wh-p?" is a "who"-question – say, of the form "who did X?" – A may know of a certain person under some descriptions that he did X, but not under other descriptions.

If the statements (a)–(c) are all true, then it is possible for A to know that q without its being the case that A can rehearse reasons, or at least adequate reasons, for q. For the sorts of conditions mentioned in (a) do not necessarily imply anything, or anything very substantial, about A's *consciousness* of reasons for q, or of his own relation to the truth of q. They are conditions *about* A, rather than conditions *on* A; we may call them (to use a phrase I owe to discussion with Mr G. O'Hare) *external* conditions. If (a)–(c) are true, then the satisfaction of such external conditions can, together with true belief, be sufficient for knowledge.

3. *Knowledge without reasons*

One might hope that it would be so. For if we consider the classical tripartite analysis of propositional knowledge, namely that A knows that p if and only if (i) p is true, (ii) A believes that p, (iii) A has good reasons for p, there is a notorious difficulty, that a regress is likely to be generated, and in more than one way.[1] For if A's reason for

---

[1] The difficulty has been well discussed by Gettier: see his article reprinted in Phillips Griffiths, ed., *Knowledge and Belief*, Oxford 1967; and also Griffiths' introduction to that

p is constituted by some other proposition which supports p, then it seems that this in turn must be something that A knows, unless we are to embrace the not very inviting conclusion that the difference between true belief and knowledge is basically the difference between believing one true thing and believing two true things which are connected. Moreover, the fact that this other proposition supports p must itself (it seems) be something that A knows, which generates a further regress.

Some formulations of the third condition (such as Ayer's "A has the right to be sure" in *The Problem of Knowledge*) are designed to be general enough to allow of at least some cases in which the appropriate grounding of A's true belief does not take the form of another proposition which A knows or believes. But the purpose of such attempts has generally been to accommodate some class or classes of propositions which supposedly possess some specially evident or ground-level character: the regress is to be stopped by *foundations*. Whatever may be said about the foundations of knowledge, I do not believe that they are thus to be brought in, as an answer to this difficulty in relation to the account of what knowledge in general is. Rather, we should acknowledge that if we are speaking *in general* about knowledge, not only is it not necessary that the knower be able to support or ground his true belief by reference to other propositions, but it is not necessary that he be in any special state with regard to this belief at all, at least at the level of what he can consciously rehearse. What is necessary – and what represents the undoubted fact that knowledge differs from mere true belief – is that one or more of a class of conditions should obtain, which relate the fact that A has this belief to the fact that the belief is true: conditions which can best be summarised by the formula that, given the truth of p, it is no accident that A believes p rather than not-p. This formula is vague and over-generous, but it gets us, I think, on the right line; in particular, in the consideration that the notion of its being "no accident" is basically the same notion as is employed in a causal investigation.

Suppose a spiritualist medium or some such is thought to have clairvoyant powers. She makes claims, of which she is convinced, about the whereabouts of certain objects, or states of affairs elsewhere. Let us suppose that her claims are clear and determinate and, moreover, true. Two questions might now be raised: is it just an accident, extraordinary good luck on her part, that she is right in

book. The present discussion is also indebted to Martin and Deutscher, "Remembering", *Philosophical Review* 1966.

this series of cases? and – does she know? My thesis is that these are the *same* question. If we are convinced that it cannot just be luck, that the probability of chance success at this level is vanishingly small, then the question arises of how the success comes about: which is the same question as, how does she know? (The difference in English, that we ask why he believes, but how does he know, a difference remarked by Austin and other philosophers, is indeed indicative of a truth.) Perhaps we shall not be able to find out how it happens: in that case, we shall not be able to tell how she knows. If we are left in that position, we shall not (*pro tanto*) be led to deny that she knows, any more than we shall deny that the correlation indeed exists, is too good for chance, and demands an explanation. We shall just be left with the admittedly puzzling fact that she does know, but there is an utter obscurity about how she knows.

We may take also a familiar real-life example. Someone in close relations with another may often know how the other feels, what thought has occurred to them, how they are about to react, why they reacted in a certain way. Their grounds for these convictions are often, at the conscious level, virtually non-existent or at least hopelessly unspecific. But if it is true that such a person is usually right – and not, as sometimes, merely passing over the negative instances – then we have little hesitation in ascribing knowledge. In this case, we also have a general idea of how they know: there is an explanatory schema available, which could in principle be further filled in, no doubt, by careful investigation of what they are subsconciously "going on."

It is worth saying in passing that the existence of such unreasoned knowledge; the existence, further (though this is not the present point) of personal and social knowledge which the subject cannot even adequately express, let alone justify: these things do not stand opposed, in some mystical way, to a rational and scientific picture of what the world is like. That humans can understand the human in ways in which the non-human is not to be understood, does not show that man stands apart from nature, but rather shows something about what kind of system in nature he is. To think, moreover, that unless unreasoned human understanding is magic, it must be possible to *replace* it with articulate and reasoned procedures in a scientific style, is again a *non-sequitur*, and in good part a scientistic illusion. To insist on thinking about personal situations in such terms makes, after all, a concrete psychological difference to the thinker, a difference which may perfectly well destroy, without replacing, the knowledge he would otherwise have. The role and importance of the reflective and self-conscious in human affairs is indeed a serious issue, but it is not to be thought of in terms of replacing weather-magic with meteorology.

4. *The difficulty of producing a criterion*

I claim, then, that it is not a requirement *in general* on knowledge that the knower be in some special conscious state in relation to his true belief; the requirement rather is that it be no accident, granted the truth of p, that he believe p rather than not-p. But if this is considered as an *analysis* of knowledge, there is no doubt that it will not serve, since it is too vague and (on natural interpretations) over-generous. For suppose that A, being from Guinea, tells B falsely that he is from Ghana; but (let us fancifully suppose) owing to features of A's spoken English which are peculiar to Guineans, B takes him to have said "Guinea" when he said "Ghana." Then B has come truly to believe that A is from Guinea, and (in an obvious sense) it is no accident, relative to A's being from Guinea, that this has come about; but B can scarcely be said to have acquired knowledge in this way, as opposed (for instance) to a situation in which, familiar with the Guinean accent, he sees through the pretence. Or again, the firm's accountant, being depressed over personal matters, is influenced by that to give a gloomy picture of the firm's affairs. The manager is depressed by this account; being disposed, when depressed, to think that everyone else is, he forms the (true) belief that the ac-countant is. This can hardly count as the acquisition of knowledge, either.

These, and other, cases do seem to be counter-examples to the "no accident" account taken without further restriction as an analysis, since they do seem (unless we covertly assume some unexplained restriction) to satisfy the general condition that the acquisition of the belief was no accident relative to its truth, and yet these are not cases of knowledge. Further investigation may be hoped to provide some appropriate types of restriction, such as those needed to dis-tinguish the passage of a piece of information (in a propositional sense – not in the generalized sense used e.g. in the biological sciences, though that is not irrelevant), from the more general notion of a causal chain with the same proposition at each end of it. In the absence of the required restrictions, I offer the "no accident" clause not as part of an analysis but (as I said before) as a label for a class of conditions, the general requirements on which need to be spelled out with greater precision.

One general requirement indeed is that the route from fact to belief should *in general* be a truth-producing or truth-preserving route – that beliefs engendered by this *kind* of process should have a good probability of being true. But that, while correct, does not actually get us very far. For the difficult question remains: at what level of generality of description is a process or kind of process to be determined to have or lack the truth-producing feature? Or – another way of putting it – what is to count as the same, or a different, process? Thus it may be said with regard to the two cases just described, that what is wrong is that the processes of belief-production involved – mishearing in the one case, being influenced by a mood in the other – are not in general truth-producing processes. Well, regarded at this level of generality, they are not. But regarded at a more specific level, with the distinctive features of the cases put in, they are, and the question is why the first and not the second level of description should properly represent our view of the situation.

Very similar problems arise with the characterization of *reasons*. A fact which, described at one level, constitutes a good reason for believing something (e.g. "being told by Jones, a reliable authority") will have many other descriptions under which it will appear as a bad reason, or no reason at all ("being told by somebody," "being told by a man who has never been to Paris"). This unsurprising parallelism between the problems of finding the right application of "no accident," and the problems of assessing reasons, is one of several grounds for supposing that the sort of difficulty presented by these cases is not one of principle with the "no accident" account, but only demands refinement of it.

5. *The place of reasons*

None of this is to deny that the possession of reasons plays an important role in the economy of the concept of knowledge. It would be highly paradoxical if there were no such role. But the present account enables us to see the nature and point of that role more clearly than does an account which merely insists on the possession of reasons.

In many cases, it will be highly probable, and in some cases, it will be necessary, that the only way in which a subject could reliably and (relative to the truth) non-accidentally acquire true beliefs is via the *thought* of considerations which support the truth-claim, that is to say, via reasons. It is likely to be so with knowledge of matters remote to the subject in space and time; though here it is worth remembering the platitude that we all possess information about the past (and leaving aside the special case of our own pasts) which is rightly accepted as knowledge, yet whose credentials lie in no ade-

quate reasons that we can muster for these propositions, but in the
"external" fact that we have acquired the information from pre-
sumptively reliable sources, which we cannot now, usually, remember.

A special sort of requirement for reasons comes into view with
propositions of certain logical types. Concerning mathematical propositions, for instance, save of the simplest kind, there is strong
pressure behind the Platonic view that the distinction between
knowledge and true belief lies in the possession of an *aitias logismos*,
a chain of proof. Plato himself claimed (at least in the *Meno*) that the
point of this demand, and thereby the superiority of knowledge, lay
in the greater permanence of beliefs so tied down. It may or may not
be psychologically true that such beliefs are more permanent, but it
hardly goes to the heart of the matter, which is surely more the point
that the access to mathematical truth must necessary lie through
proof, and that therefore the notion of non-accidental true belief in
mathematics essentially involves the notion of mathematical proof
(the points which the Platonic model of *recollection* precisely serves
to obscure).

Now I can truly believe a mathematical proposition, which I
cannot demonstrate, because I have been authoritatively told that
it is true. This would be widely agreed not to constitute knowledge
– knowledge, that is, that p, where p is the mathematical proposition.
But there is another piece of knowledge that I might well be said
to have in these same circumstances – the knowledge that p is a
mathematical truth. It will seem paradoxical to take apart in any
way knowing that p, and knowing that p is true. But if these two are
kept logically tied together, then the line must come between knowing that p is true, and knowing that p is a truth of a given science.
To be a truth of a given science is to be, in a special sense, a part of
knowledge; and to know that a proposition has that status is to know
that it is, by the standards of that science, to be counted as *known*,
as opposed to its being, for instance, a matter merely of plausible
conjecture.

This consideration brings us to a last and different sort of connection between knowledge and reasons. So far, I have been discussing knowledge as, in a certain sense and in part, a psychological
concept, one to be applied to individuals with respect to their hold
on true propositions. But there is such a thing as impersonal knowledge, as when we speak of the state of knowledge in a given field, or
of something's now being known which was not known 20 years ago,
or of the structure of a certain molecule not being known though
there exist various theories or hypotheses about it.

That there should be radically impersonal knowledge seems, on the face of it, impossible: if p is known, then somebody surely must know it. But this apparent platitude is in conflict with other things we are also disposed to accept, and at least one of them has got to give. Let "Kip" stand for "it is known that p," in the sense under discussion, and "Kap" stand for "a knows that p." The apparent platitude is

(1) If Kip, then, for some a, Kap.

The following, further, seems to be plausible:

(2) If Kip and Kiq, then Ki(p & q).

But certainly this is not true:

(3) If Kip and Kiq, then, for some a, Ka(p & q);

If (3) were true, the age of the universal polymath would not be behind us. But (3) is entailed by (1) and (2), since "p & q" will of course be a substitution instance of "p" in (1). I will not explore this problem here, beyond pointing out that we must resist the temptation to defend (1) on the basis of the two assumptions (a) that the logic of "Kip" will be revealed by concentrating just on true assertions of the form "Kip," (b) that anyone who truly asserts or, at least, who *knows*, that Kip must himself know that p. Neither is true. A proper understanding of "Kip" will take into account for instance, questions whether Kip; and as to (b), we have already seen in the mathematical case that it is false.

I have mentioned this problem only to show that the relations between impersonal and personal knowledge are not as simple as may at first appear. Now, impersonal knowledge certainly has a special commitment to reasons. Bodies of knowledge are essentially, if to varying degrees with different subjects, systematic. There is both a pure and an applied reason for this. Pure, because the aim is not just to know but to understand, and in scientific cases at least understanding necessarily implies organization and economy. Applied, because a body of knowledge will only be freely extensible and open to criticism if rationally organized. And there are of course other considerations which support the same point. So knowledge, in this sense, must have reasons. It may, even, have foundations, though that is an open question. What it is an open question *of*, however, is the philosophy of science; these are different issues from those of epistemology in general, that is to say, the study of knowledge as such, and in particular personal knowledge.

Whatever is to be said about the relations between personal and impersonal knowledge, it is of course true that what is known is fragmentarily known by various persons; the *savant* has internalized some part of a body of knowledge. Insofar as this is true, his personal knowledge will satisfy the standards of rational organization which are appropriate to a body of knowledge. But we must not take that special case as *the* clue to the account we should give of the ordinary business of personal knowledge.

A. J. AYER

(*University of Oxford*)

COMMENTS ON PROFESSOR WILLIAMS'
"KNOWLEDGE AND REASONS"

My remarks on Professor Williams' paper will be relatively brief, both because I think that the opener of the discussion should be brief, and because I am in substantial agreement with what Professor Williams has said. In the first place, I accept his distinction between propositional and practical knowledge, and I too shall have nothing to say about practical knowledge. I agree with him that the labels which Ryle used to mark this distinction are not quite satisfactory, and I think that his use of the formula "A knows wh-p," in the propositional case, is an improvement on Ryle's "knowing that." I think he is right in saying that one narrows the problem unduly, if one concentrates only on true assertions of the form "it is known that p," and I agree that from the fact that a person A knows that some proposition p is known it does not follow that A himself knows that p.

Williams suggests that someone who did assume, mistakenly, that "A knows that p" followed from "A knows that it is known that p" might be led by this assumption to accept the proposition that if p is known, then for some person A, A knows that p. Let us call this proposition H. Williams does not explicitly reject H, but he thinks it open to doubt and is therefore willing to entertain the possibility of what he calls "radically impersonal knowledge." But here I believe that he may have gone astray. His reason for thinking that H may be false is that in conjunction with the proposition "If p is known and q is known, p and q are known," which would seem to be true, it entails the undoubtedly false proposition "If p is known and q is known, then for some person A, A knows that p and q." This entailment is said by him to hold in virtue of the fact that "p and q" is a substitution instance of "p" in the proposition H. But the trouble here is that there is an ambiguity in the expression "p is known"; and once this ambiguity is removed, there is no longer any puzzle. If "p is known" is construed, in the way I think it should be, as being equivalent to "for some person A, A knows wh-p," then Williams' second premiss is false. It may well be the case that someone knows wh-p and that someone knows wh-q without its being the case that any one person knows wh-p and q. On the other hand, if "p is known" is taken, in the way that Williams presumably intends, as being equivalent to "p is part of the corpus of human knowledge," then there is no question but that H itself is false. The assumption that nothing can be an item of knowledge unless some person knows it does indeed sound plausible, but it ceases to be plausible once any amount of knowledge is allowed to count as a single item.

The fact that H is false, when it is understood in this way, is, however, an insufficient reason for speaking of there being radically impersonal knowledge. This is not, after all, a peculiarity about knowing; it applies just as much to loving or to eating: if Tom is loved and Bill is loved, it does not follow that any one person loves them both; if caviar is being eaten and peanuts are being eaten, it does not follow that any one person is eating them both: yet this would hardly entitle us to talk of there being a radically impersonal love or a radically impersonal consumption of food. Williams himself draws the proper conclusion when he says, in his last paragraph, that what is known, in the sense here in question, is fragmentarily known by different persons. If he meant no more than this by his talk of impersonal knowledge, I have no quarrel with him, but I have the impression that he did mean something more.

Perhaps what he had in mind was a distinction which is both valid and important. This is the distinction between knowledge considered impersonally as a body of generally accepted doctrine, without regard to the biographies of those who possess it, and knowledge considered as an individual acquisition. In the first of these cases, as Williams recognizes, reasons are all important. We are concerned with the questions how the different elements in the given body of doctrine are logically related, how one item can support another when the relation between them falls short of logical entailment, what foundations there are for the whole system. In the second case, we are interested in personal credentials. Reasons come into it here also, in that a claim to know some proposition may be upheld by claiming to know another proposition which supports it, but, as Williams rightly points out, this is not the only way in which such claims are upheld.

There is no doubt, to my mind, that the first of these two approaches is philosophically much the more interesting. The credentials of propositions are a more rewarding study than the credentials of persons. It is, however, also true that if we are considering knowledge impersonally, there is little point in making any very strenuous effort to distinguish it from belief. With the possible exception of the individual's monitoring of his own immediate experience, which does not as such enter into the stock of public knowledge, all our opinions about matters of fact are fallible and open to revision; and the question at what point a proposition becomes so well-entrenched that it is correct to speak of its being not merely believed but known to be true is not of any great importance. It will, in any case, be a matter of degree. What a schoolmaster teaches and expects his pupils to know is the body of theory that is generally accepted in his day: it would be pedantic of him to refuse to call it knowledge, on the ground of the likelihood that some of it will no longer be accepted in a hundred years time. Neither do we value knowledge, or what we count as knowledge, in proportion to its security. Scientific theories are less secure than most of what we regard as the facts of history, but they are of greater cognitive utility. Carlyle once said that he would surrender the whole of science for one solid fact, like "John Lackland took this road." To which Henri Poincaré gave the scientist's reply: "Of what interest is that, since he will not be taking it again?"

No doubt it is its combination of security with generality that has prompted many philosophers, from Plato onwards, to look on mathematics as the paradigm of knowledge. In Plato's case, this led to an attempt to distinguish knowledge from belief by differentiating between their objects. But this is surely misguided. In so far as the distinction between what Hume called "relations of ideas" and "matters of fact" is tenable at all, there are other ways of making it: we can talk of the distinction between the a priori and the a posteriori, or between the analytic and the synthetic, or between the necessary and the contingent. I am not here committing myself to saying that these distinctions exactly coincide, or even implying that any one of them is well made out. My point is only that there is no call to add the distinction between knowledge and belief to their list. Not only would this have the effect of giving the concept of knowledge an unduly narrow extension, but it would also bestow a false security upon the propositions of mathematics. From the fact, if it be a fact, that mathematical propositions are necessary, it by no means follows that we have an infallible intuition of their truth. One hopes that set theory has been entirely freed from contradiction, but it would be rash to assume that no such crisis as that which Frege faced when Russell's discovery of the class-paradox was communicated to him, could ever again occur.

Among empirical propositions, the most secure are those that express judgments of inner or outer perception; and the smaller their content, the greater their security. Those with minimal content are a person's reports of his present thoughts, feelings, or sensations; it remains a contested question whether such reports can be factually mistaken, but, as I hinted earlier, I think it arguable that they cannot be. But then, as I also said, propositions of this kind are not represented in the corpus of what Williams calls impersonal knowledge. That I am at this moment having such and such feelings or am confronted with such and such sense-qualia is not a fact of any general interest. Judgements of perception are, indeed, important, not individually but as a class, in that they collectively supply the evidence on which our knowledge of the world is founded. Even so, when we present this evidence, we are normally content to describe features of the world which we have discovered to be observable, rather than to list the occasions on which they have actually been observed.

On the topic of knowledge, considered personally, I have little to add to what Williams has said. I think, as he does, that there are various different grounds on which claims to knowledge can be accredited, and I therefore suspect that if one is trying to define knowledge, in its personal aspect, one may have to be content with some such vague formula as my own "having the right to be sure." If one ventures on anything more precise, one is likely to be faced with counter-examples. For instance, Williams remarks, quite correctly, that someone who has followed his usual practice of consulting the railway time-table can, in the normal way, be properly said to know when the train is due to start. But it might happen that he misread the time-table and still got the right answer, because the time of the train's departure had been changed to that which his misreading yielded and in those circumstances we should not want to say that he knew when the train was due to start. No doubt cases of this kind are covered by Williams' formula that it should be no accident that the man's belief is true; but how is this formula to be made both concrete and watertight? One might think of making it a necessary condition for knowledge that one's belief in what one claims to know should not be causally dependent on a false belief, but this would be too stringent. For instance, it may well be the case that one of the causes of my now believing that the Battle of Hastings was fought in 1066 was a childish belief that the schoolmaster who first imparted this piece of knowledge to me was a man whose word could universally be trusted. Now this belief may easily have been false; yet it would not ordinarily be thought to follow that I could not know when the Battle of Hastings was fought.

No doubt this suggestion could be refined upon, but I am sceptical of its power to yield a precise formula which would differentiate between knowledge and true belief in a way that we found generally acceptable. I am indeed not convinced that any such formula is discoverable. We are usually able to decide the question in particular cases, though even here there may be differences of opinion, but I have some doubt whether these particular decisions can be fitted tidily under any general rule. As I remarked earlier, the distinction is anyhow one of degree and the question how it should be drawn, to correspond as closely as possible with customary usage, is perhaps one of those linguistic questions that are not of major philosophical importance.

E. J. Furlong

(*University of Dublin*)

MEMORY RE-CHAINED

Introduction

In his ably-argued and provocative paper "Memory unchained" (*Philosophical Review*, April 1969), Mr Roger Squires attempts to refute what I shall term a causal theory of memory, and he provides an alternative account. He uses analogies of the kind, "a sack of grain in the granary in January is not operative in producing the same bag of grain in the granary for the rest of the year" (p. 196); rather, the sack exists now, in August, because it has existed all along. So likewise, he argues, if I remember a visit to the University of Tbilisi five years ago (the example is mine) – a visit, events in which are still fresh in my memory – my recollection is to be explained, not by some supposed causal linkage between then and now, but rather by my retaining, over the five years, a certain ability.

(My visit to the University of Tbilisi is, I should explain here, stamped in my memory by a number of incidents: for example, after the colleague who accompanied me and I had discussed with the friendly Rector and some professors why Russian girls were so good at mathematics, or kindred university topics, somewhat laboriously on a warm September afternoon, with the aid of Russian and Georgian interpreters, the Rector turned to me and remarked gently in perfectly good English, "You know I visited Dublin a few years ago for a conference.")

A theory explicitly requiring a causal chain had been advanced, also in the *Philosophical Review* (April 1966), by C. B. Martin and Max Deutscher. Their article is a main target for attack by Squires. I shall have something to say about their views later in this paper.

Squires' account of memory, I note *en passant*, is typical of a familiar line of argument in contemporary British philosophy, and perhaps also in other traditions, the attempt to replace explanations in terms of (possibly hidden) occurrences by explanations in terms of dispositions, or of observable behaviour.

In what follows I shall, to avoid an excessive appearance of controversy, refer for the most part, not to Squires' discussion directly, though I shall have his arguments very much in mind. The positive view of memory which he defends may, I think, be adequately termed the Persisting Ability Theory; and by this name I shall refer to the view in the following discussion.

The Persisting Ability Theory considered

Let us first dispose of a preliminary issue. Take my Tbilisi visit. If I am to remember this experience I must certainly retain something, to speak broadly, from the original occasion. But it might well be added that, if I am to claim validly to remember the visit, I must be able to recall it. There must be retention, and there must, it would obviously seem, be the ability to recall. Both elements would appear to be of equal importance. Neither is the junior partner. As against this view, however, it is sometimes argued (by e.g. Squires) that retaining is central, whereas recall is marginal. That thesis cannot, I think, be accepted. It would, for example, be very odd to say, I remember my visit quite well, only I cannot recall it; or to say, I remember your name clearly, though I cannot call it to mind. Rather, we say, for example, I cannot remember that man's name, though it is on the tip of my tongue.

It follows, therefore, that the question we are to discuss is a question not only about an ability to retain but also about an ability to recall. The question will be, how do I account for my holding on to the name, or to my Tbilisi visit, so that I can recall the item when required?

We may usefully now consider the sack-of-grain analogy. "A sack of grain in the granary in January is not operative in producing the same bag of grain in the granary for the rest of the year." That is true, but it is not the whole truth. If the sack of grain is to persist, then, as a physicist would tell us, there must be what we might call a causal commerce between the sack and its surroundings: the elementary particles of the sack are in constant interaction with their environment. A physiologist would provide a parallel account of memory: particles of my nervous system are in constant causal commerce with their environment. A change in my nervous system brought about by my visit to Tbilisi is incorporated in this commerce, and plays a necessary part in accounting for my ability to remember the incident (i.e. to retain and to recall).

A better analogy to memory here than the sack of grain would be the persistence of a population. How, for example, do we account for the existence of the present Finnish population of Helsinki? The historian will tell us that a Finnish people arrived in this locality about 1640. By a process of constant interaction with their environment, a human geographer could add, they have survived to inhabit the present city. The same persons, of course, have not survived; but the present citizens are nevertheless causally linked, through the continuing commerce, with the inhabitants of 1640.

This account, the account given by the historian and the geographer, is the kind of account that would satisfy us. We should hardly feel happy if we were told that the Finnish people are here because they have been here all along.

Likewise with memory. It is hardly enough to be told that I can now remember my visit to Georgia because I could remember it all along. What, I reasonably ask, has enabled me to remember it all along – on 1 January 1968, 1 January 1969, 1 April 1970? Here the causal commerce provides, I submit, the item needed if a satisfactory explanation is to be given.

The memory trace

I referred above to the article "Remembering" by Martin and Deutscher. Their declared aim is to provide an adequate definition of memory, a definition that will exclude cases of non-memory and include all cases that would be commonly regarded as memory. Ingenious invention of counter-examples, combined with resourceful modification, leads them to consider the role in recall of prompting, by, say, a companion or a diary. To cope with a recherché objection they introduce as a necessary element in their definition the memory trace. The memory trace is a "structural analogue of what was experienced."

What Martin and Deutscher have to say about the memory trace corresponds in essentials to what has been said above about a causal commerce, a commerce by means of which – as with the inhabitants of Helsinki – a modification brought about by a past event persists through change.

The memory trace, as might be expected, is closely scrutinised – and severely handled – by Squires. He asks, in particular, "What is to stop us from regarding the memory trace itself as a prompt, producing the absurd conclusion that we never remember anything?" (p. 195). He considers, but rejects, as a possible answer, the suggestion that prompts are observed whereas traces are not. I do not find his rejection of this answer convincing; and if the arguments he uses were in fact effective they should, I think, apply with equal force in the case of sense-perception. We should, if his arguments were sound, be equally at a loss to explain the difference between a man viewing a crowd scene for himself from a window – in consequence of light-rays, nervous processes, etc., all unobserved, and his being prompted by an (observed) commentary to visualise it.

Defining and telling the difference

Nevertheless Squires' criticism does suggest a matter of principle about the problem of definition that Martin and Deutscher set themselves to solve. I might make the point I have in mind by an analogy. Suppose that I am seeking to define the object, cat. A zoologist friend tells me that a cat is a retractile-clawed quadruped of the species *felis domesticus*. (This, I understand, is less than adequate as a scientific definition, but I am assured that it is on the right lines – and it will suit my purpose.) My friend's definition might prompt me to comment that, however scientifically proper it may be, it might not help me to decide whether the strange, shaggy, hungry-looking creature on my doorstep is a cat or some odd kind of dog: the nervous animal angrily repels my attempts to discover whether its claws are, or are not, retractile. What I am, however, able with less difficulty to test is whether the creature purrs when stroked. Here I have a more helpful attribute than the practically unobservable quality, retractile-clawed. My scientific friend might agree: he might say that as a matter of fact cats, and only cats, among quadrupeds, purr when stroked. But all the same, he might add, I do not choose to put that quality into my definition. To this I might reply, I am sure you have your reasons, but nevertheless, when it comes to telling the difference, I opt for purring.

Now it seems to me that, correct as Martin and Deutscher may be when they include the memory trace in their definition of memory, their account might leave a reader still asking the question – and in a way this is what Squires is doing – how can I tell when I am remembering? To that question there is, I think, in fact a commonsense and practical answer, analogous to the purring test for the cat. When I call to mind my visit to Tbilisi I am confident that this is memory, and not, say, concoction, fiction, by *inter alia* the fact that as Hume said, the incident "flows in upon the mind in a forcible manner": I believe that the incident occurred: I assent to its occurrence. (Martin and Deutscher discount this element of belief; but I think they have not reckoned with the fact that belief admits of degrees – from absolute conviction to a fragile inclination to accept, and that the accompanying memory may *pari passu* vary in clarity and assurance.)

When referring to Hume just now I used the phrase *"inter alia."* I did so to take account of the fact that, as is often remarked, we sometimes find introspective criteria inadequate or unreliable, and are compelled to supplement them by recourse to the evidence of diaries and other such records. Nevertheless, there are cases where the introspective criterion can be quite compelling. Thus it happened to me that I was trying vainly to recall the name of the person, commonly considered to be the founder of the Vienna Circle. "Carnap?" No, "Neurath?" No. "Schlick?" Yes, that is it. The search is ended. Eureka! It's the key that opens the lock. I readily give my assent; indeed I cannot withhold it.

A final consideration

To support a causal account I shall offer in conclusion a consideration from an area of enquiry in which some philosophers busied themselves a decade or two ago. It was then asserted, perhaps still is, by some thinkers that there is respectable, laboratory evidence for pre-cognition. Professor Rhine, of Duke University, and others claimed that experiments with cards produce, with certain persons, results whose correctness is quite inexplicable by chance. These persons can foresee what card is going to be turned up in, say, two minutes' time.

I do not need to discuss here whether these claims are valid or not: I wish only to recall one reaction of philosophers who reflected on these claims some fifteen years ago. A question they asked was this: supposing a person can precognise, how does he do it? If, they noted, we have the experience of seeing a brown table in front of us, there is, we believe, a related scientific account: particles of light reflected from a scientifically described object reach our eyes, brain changes occur, and we see. The physical changes are a condition of our seeing. Likewise, they said, in the case of memory. Must we, they then re-marked, not similarly discover some causal link between the turning up of the card and the precogniser's awareness of this event? But how, they asked, could such a causal process occur? An ace of spades is turned up at two minutes past ten. At ten the precogniser is aware that this is the card to be turned up. The effect apparently precedes the cause. This is impossible – or is it? Suppose time had two di-mensions, or suppose we expanded our concept of cause ... I do not have to dwell on the ingenious speculations which resourceful thinkers then entertained. This demand sprang from what seemed to them obvious – needing no argument – namely, that causal accounts are required and available in the case of memory – and, of course, sense-perception. What is true for the past – and the present –

must also be true, they argued, for the future. They witnessed, therefore, incidentally, to the belief that the causal element is an ingredient
in a satisfactory account of memory.

Postscript

The stress I have laid on the causal element has a bearing on a
general comment that might be made on my discussion, namely that
I have failed to keep apart two questions, (a) what is it to remember?
and (b) how, in fact, do we remember? Martin and Deutscher, it
might be said, are concerned with the first question, Squires with the
second, and therefore (possibly) the conflict between them is unreal.
To this comment I would reply, first, that Squires certainly thinks
he and those he is criticising are concerned with the same question:
he does explicitly oppose what he terms a causal theory of memory.
But, more importantly, the two questions, cannot, I think, be held
apart. The answer to the question, what is it to remember? e.g. to
remember, rather than to fabricate, my Georgian visit, includes, if,
following Martin and Deutscher, I am right, a reference to the me-
mory-trace, i.e. includes an answer to the question, how in fact do we
remember? And the person who raises the question, how do we
remember? is presuming that he knows what it is to remember.

It might also be said that the meaningful question to ask is not,
how do we remember this or that? but rather, why is it that we
remember one thing and fail to remember another? i.e. a specific
question rather than a general one. I admit that the latter question
is often of interest, but I do not see that it rules out the propriety of
the general question. In the same way it might be asked, how is it
that dogs can sometimes hear sounds that are inaudible to human
beings? This specific question does not however rule out the general
question, how do we hear? how is hearing done? to which an answer
in terms of sound-waves, eardrums, etc. can be given.

Summary

I have attempted to defend a causal account of memory as against
what I have termed the Persisting Ability Theory. The latter denies
that our ability to recall a past incident is causally dependent on a
past experience. I have argued that this denial should be rejected
but that nevertheless, the causal element may be of little use as a
means of telling the difference between remembering and imagining.
Here we do well to take account of such items as belief, Humean
"force" and, of course, external records and other evidence.

E D U A R D O   N I C O L

(*Université Nationale de Mexico*)

CONNAISSANCE ET RECONNAISSANCE

1. Puisque cette séance sur La Mémoire vient encadrée dans le thème général de La théorie de la Connaissance, ce n'est pas une étude monographique sur la mémoire qu'on nous propose. Il s'agirait plutôt d'examiner si la mémoire participe nécessairement aux opérations de la connaissance.

D'abord, on pourrait croire qu'elle n'y participe pas, et les études psychologiques, voire philosophiques, s'accorderaient en général sur ce point. N'importe comment soit conçue la fonction de la mémoire, ses actes ne seraient pas ceux d'une connaissance actuelle.

Bien entendu, l'exercice de la mémoire présuppose toujours une connaissance actuelle; mais, pour devenir un objet de la mémoire, le connu doit perdre justement son actualité: il doit être d'abord relegué au passé. Il y a aussi une connaissance du passé qui ne peut être qu'actuelle, et qui fournit la substance de l'expérience humaine, de la tradition, de la science historique. Sans la mémoire, ces modalités spécifiques de la connaissance ne seraient pas possibles. Mais cela confirmerait plutôt que la mémoire opère seulement sur le dejà connu, et qu'elle contribue comme auxilaire à une connaissance de deuxième degré.

Le souvenir ne serait donc qu'une literale re-connaissance, qu'une re-actualisation: une opération qui nous permet de transporter à l'actualité ce que nous savons trés bien, par la nécessité même de ce transport, qu'il n'appartient de son droit au présent. La vraie connaissance, au contraire, celle de premier degré, ne porterait que sur le présent, sur ce qui est là: la donnée inmédiate.

Tout ceci est sans doute vrai, mais pas tout à fait. Il ne serait peut-être pas inutile d'explorer les composants de cette connaissance actuelle, en vue d'identifier parmi eux une coopération de la mémoire. On peut anticiper que, si le resultat de cette analyse est positif, les consequences de la vérification ne manqueront pas d'une importance philosophique générale.

2. En étudiant la mémoire, nous sommes enclins à la considérer comme une fonction ou faculté qui produit des actes isolés. Ces actes, que nous appelons les souvenirs, se produisent quelques fois automatiquement, par les ressorts de l'association; d'autres fois, c'est la volonté qui dirige notre attention au déjà vecu. Dans les deux situations, il y a quelque chose qui déclenche soudainement ce mécanisme du souvenir, lequel nous permet de transposer le temps passé au présent. Une fois accomplie cette opération de mélange des temps, pour l'appeler ainsi, la conscience reviendrait aux actualités. Dans ce siège de notre existence qui serait la présent pur, rien ne requiert, en apparence, du concours de la mémoire.

Mais est-ce qu'il existe vraiment ce présent pur? Pur voudrait dire: sans mélange du passé.

Si la mémoire est bien la faculté spécifique de la temporalité humaine, il n'est pas concévable qu'elle soit une faculté d'action intermittente. Mais ce n'est pas seulement la retention qui est continuelle. Le souvenir doit être toujours présent, pour qu'on puisse avoir le sens même du présent. On peut affirmer sans paradoxe que le présent ne se distingue du passé que par l'incorporation du passé dans le présent.

Tout le monde reconnait que la continuité temporelle n'est pas celle d'une progression en ligne droite qui marquerait un mouvement irréversible. Mais, sans y réfléchir, nous détachons le présent, comme si le passé et le futur, le souvenir et l'anticipation, n'eussent qu'une place occasionelle dans un présent déjà constitué. Celui-ci reste alors artificiellement privé de sa temporalité. En effet, quand nous lui attribuons une limite précise, le présent se paralise, il devient statique. C'est ainsi que nous prétendons alors le saisir comme pur présent: comme le domaine exclusif du *hic et nunc.*

Personne ne peut plus douter que le présent est, lui-même, une continuité sans coupure et sans arrêt. On doit prêter attention spéciale au passé immédiat. Nous constatons qu'il y a une liaison entre le soi-disant présent pur et ce qui vient tout justement de devenir le passé. Ce passé immédiat persiste dans le présent et c'est la mémoire toujours active qui produit cette persistance. Sans la continuité du souvenir (ce qui signifie: sans cette *actualité constante du passé*), le présent pur n'est qu'une absurde abstraction: il deviendrait pour chacun une sorte de nouveauté totale, decoupée du courant de la vie.

Nous ne pouvons assigner au présent des limites définies. La distinction entre le présent et le passé est nécessaire pour la conceptuation de l'estructure de la temporalité, et elle est bien fondée sur la realité du vecu. Dans le concret de l'expérience, ces limites restent indeterminées. La rétention ne consiste pas à préserver le dejà vecu hors de présent, comme dans un archive. On dirait plutôt que c'est l'oubli qui, pour l'économie de l'existence, pousse le dejà vecu hors de présent. Primordialement, le mémoire retient le passé dans le présent, pour que celui-ci puisse couler sans arrêt. Ce qui revient à dire tout simplement que la connaissance *actuelle* est elle-même un courant, et que, par consequent, la mémoire ne doit pas être conçue ni comme une fonction intermittente, ni comme une faculté de l'inactuel.

3. Nous pouvons néanmoins nous demander pourquoi ce qui est là ne suffirait-il pas à former une conscience pleine du présent actuel.

On affirme aisement que le souvenir est une re-connaissance. Il faudrait ajouter que toute connaissance est une re-connaissance; donc, qu'elle implique un souvenir.

Limitons-nous, par concision, à la connaissance perceptive. Si nous pouvions imaginer qu'un objet réel se présente pour la première fois devant nous avec les caractères d'une nouveauté absolue, la simple apprehension de sa présence ne constituerait proprement une connaissance. Nous pourrions même douter de la realité de cet objet: de son *objectivité*. Car, par sa nouveauté même, cette chose singulière demeurerait ontologiquement et epistemologiquement dé-pourvue de toute connection avec quelque chose de distinct (précise-ment parce qu'elle serait tellement distincte); elle n'entrerait en relation avec aucune de nos expériences antérieures; enfin, nous ne pourrions dire d'elle absolument rien. Ce mutisme est la clé de la situation. Car de ce qui est, on peut toujours dire quelque chose.

Or, la seconde fois qu'un tel objet se présenterait, tout en restant également inconnu, il serait cependant reconnu; nous dirions de cet chose qu'elle est "la même." Notre re-présentation partirait de cette nouvelle présentation. Le souvenir aurait fourni le nécéssaire pour une préliminaire objectivation.

La connaissance de n'importe quel objet requiert, comme con-dition de son objectivité, la notion plus ou moins claire, mais efficace, de son ipseité. L'être est présence; mais il n'y a pas de présence sans persistance. Donc, *pas d'identification sans mémoire*. Perception et mémoire poursuivent ensemble l'être au cours de sa persistance. Exister c'est *être en cours*.

La *ousia* des grecs, que nous traduisons par substance, voulait exprimer cette persistance ou consistance de l'étant. Seulement, la métaphysique grecque (et la métaphysique traditionelle derivée d'elle) concevait la persistance comme immobilité. Pour affirmer la consistance de l'étant, on lui ôtait sa durée. La vraie connaissance était, par consequent, un acte de l'intuition, sans recours à la mémoire.

Sans tomber dans le jeux des mots, nous pouvons dire que la consistance est à la fois "ce en quoi l'étant consiste" (essence, au sens platonique) et la persistance de l'étant dans son entité propre au cours du temps. La connaissance de l'étant est, donc, un acte de la mémoire. Plus exactement: un acte qui ne s'achève que par le concours de la mémoire. Il est comme un temoignage de la continuité inherente à tout ce qui existe. Si rien ne persiste, disait Platon, on ne peut rien connaître. Ajoutons qu'on ne peut rien connaître non plus si la mémoire ne retient au présent les états passés de ce qui est là, *hic et nunc.*

Il est evident que les choses nouvelles qui s'offrent à nous d'ordinaire ne sont pas absolument neuves, dans un sens à la fois ontologique et epistemologique. Leur entité isolée, singulière, peut être nouvelle pour nous: cette ville, cette personne, cette table; mais nous discernons avec plus ou moins d'adresse la classe d'entités à laquelle elle appartient. C'est cela qui nous permet de reconnaître ce que nous n'avons jamais vu. Connaître c'est bien reconnaître l'inconnu, et ceci ne peut se produire sans le souvenir.

4. Insistons. Ce qui se présente à nous la première fois est identifié. Comment pouvons nous identifier, c'est à dire reconnaître, ce qui vient tout juste de se présenter, ce qui manque pour nous d'antécédents? En verité, il n'y a rien qui manque d'antécédents. Il s'agit de deux reconnaissances qui se produissent ensemble. Identifier signifie, dans ce contexte, à la fois admettre que l'objet est "le même" (et cette reconnaissance requiert la persistance de la représentation), et le reconnaître comme appartenant à une certaine classe dejà connue, donc rememorée. Ce placement préliminaire de l'objet lui prête un contour et fixe pour nous son identité. *Pas d'identification sans relation.* La première fois qu'on voit l'objet devient ainsi, par la cooperation de la mémoire, une seconde fois. Il y a un mouvement intérieur dans l'acte, en apparence simple, de l'appréhension.

On doit noter que l'objectivation n'est pas complète dans cette reconnaissance préliminaire. L'argument idéaliste, poussé jusqu'au bout, nous forcerait à admettre que cette reconnaissance se produit en somme au sein de la conscience individuelle. L'objectivité ne serait qu'une projection de la subjectivité. Mais l'objectivité accomplie n'est pas une perception, même redoublée. Elle s'achève dialogiquement, dans l'acte de participation verbale de deux sujets, pour lesquels l'objet devient *l'être commun*. En effet, chacun des deux interlocuteurs présente à l'autre cet être là, comme quelque chose de verifiable objectivement, de vraiment existant au dehors de chacune des *deux consciences* subjectives. La conscience individuelle n'est plus isolée dans le dialogue. Mais cet aspect de la question, qui touche à la fin de l'idéalisme, appartient plutôt au thème de l'évidence. Il faut indiquer seulement ici que la présentation verbale (*apophansis*) ne peut s'accomplir sans le concours de la mémoire, pas plus que la reconnaissance empirique ou sensorielle.

Addenda

Quelques remarques suggerées par la discussion qui s'engagea après la lecture du texte ci-dessus pourront peut-être aider à éclaircir quelques points.

I. Si nous concédons pour un instant (ce qui n'est pas aucunement nécessaire) que la proposition "il n'y a pas d'identification sans mémoire" n'exprime qu'un fait bien connu, c'est à dire, connu de tout le monde, nous n'en serons plus avancés dans l'analyse de l'objectivation; par contre, un nouveau problème va demander notre attention: qu'est-ce que "bien connu" peut signifier, de quelle sorte de connaissance s'agit-il? D'abord, la qualification de "bien connu," appliquée au contenu de la proposition, semble indiquer son acceptation. Il s'agirait donc d'une verité acquise. Acquise, comment et par qui? Car le "tout le monde" n'a pas un sens littéral; ce doit être le monde restreint formé par ceux qu'on appelle des savants. Il y a, par consequent, une affirmation qui n'est pas spéculative, qui n'est pas erronée, qui n'est pas non plus une verité de sens commun, et dont le seul defaut serait d'être trop acreditée.

Mais, justement, on constate que "les savants" ne font pas expressément la part de la mémoire quand ils examinent l'acte de l'objectivation, et qu'ils n'invoquent aucune raison valable pour laisser sous-entenduc cette partie primordiale de ses opérations. Devrait-on dire alors que cette verité est plutôt discreditée? Ce serait un exemple de ces verités qu'on appelle après coup bien connues, parce qu'elles étaient bien oubliées: celles qui demeurent à l'état latent, et qui ne sont vraiment connues que lorsqu'on les retrouve dans un texte qui les place dans une perspective systématique.

La pensée est un discours integré. Toutes les parties sont appelées à repondre de chacune, et ce serait une mauvaise logique celle qui démonterait cette articulation, en prétendant que chaque formule réponde toute seule d'elle même, détachée de la solidarité discoursive. Si la proposition "il n'y a pas d'identification sans mémoire" ne signifie que ceci: que toute reconnaissance implique la mémoire, alors il ne s'agit plus d'une verité acquise, mais de l'inutile banalité d'une répétition; il est *trop* evident que le terme reconnaissance présuppose une première connaissance, dont le sujet doit conserver un souvenir plus ou moins confus. Mais, au contraire, ce qu'il fallait montrer c'est un fait qui choque d'abord le sens commun, à savoir, que *toute connaissance est une reconnaissance* (dans un sens que le texte tâche de préciser). Il apparait maintenant que cette descente vers la banalité était artificielle, et ne pouvait s'accomplir qu'au moyen d'un jeu d'esprit, lui aussi bien connu, qui consiste à solliciter le texte après l'avoir cité hors du contexte. Procédé qui prend de nos jours une nouvelle tournure, lorsque le jugement negatif précède l'analyse, et celle-ci ne s'applique qu'à certaines phrases choisies *pro forma*, dans le seul but de renforcer le jugement préalable porté sur l'ensemble.

La proposition en question fait partie d'un exposé qui nous amène à plusieurs vérifications entrelacées: que l'objectivation n'est pas seulement conscience d'une présence, mais qu'elle implique une identification (provisoire, si l'on veut, ou même erronée: cela ne change rien dans l'opération, au point de vue fonctionnel); qu'il n'y a pas d'identification sans relation (relation entre deux perceptions du même objet, et surtout, relation avec d'autres objets de la même classe, ou de classes voisines); que l'objet présent est littéralement re-connu *la première fois* qu'on le voit, ce qui n'est possible que grâce à la mémoire; enfin, qu'il y a une complexité de facteurs dans l'acte, en apparence simple, de l'appréhension de l'objet. Cette appréhension n'est pas purement sensorielle.

Revenons sur le début de la question. Pourquoi aurait-on proposé le thème de la mémoire sous le titre général de la Théorie de la Connaissance? C'est bien parce qu'on croyait implicitement que la mémoire participe aux opérations gnoseologiques. Il fallait montrer comment cela se produit. Il ne s'agissait pas de mener à bout une étude monographique, dans l'espoir de découvrir quelque capacité inconnue de la mémoire, mais tout simplement d'en rélever une qui reste méconnue. Mais le fil conducteur était la connaissance, pas la mémoire. L'examen phénoménologique nous permet de saisir la relation nécessaire entre cette faculté et la perception dans la connaissance *actuelle* des objets. La portée de cette relation dépasse la psychologie (du moins, la psychologie conçue comme une des sciences naturelles). Pour la philosophie, c'est toujours un problème que d'établir les conditions de possibilité de la connaissance d'un objet qui est changeant et persistant à la fois. L'aspect ontologique et l'aspect epistémologique sont interdépendants. Or, les termes habituels du problème ne contiennent cette donnée qui est la participation de la mémoire.

Un de nos contemporains soutient que ce qu'il y a de grand et de durable dans la pensée des philosophes n'est justement rien de plus que le fait de donner parole expresse à ce dont, en tout temps, on trouvait de vagues resonnances éparses. Même si on n'accepte pas littéralement cette notion, ou si elle s'applique avec des reductions convenables, il n'en reste pas moins vrai que le discours philosophique ne s'articule jamais avec des pièces entièrement originelles, dont chacune représenterait une nouveauté sans précédents. La nouveauté (si tant est qu'on s'en soucie) peut apparaître dans une présentation systématique de certains faits plus ou moins connus. D'ailleurs, le point de départ d'une recherche est toujours une connaissance dejà acquise. L'histoire de la science montre que celle-ci n'avance pas seulement chaque fois qu'on découvre des faits nouveaux; le plus souvent, elle avance lorsqu'on réussit à rendre des faits connus une raison qui restait inconnue.

Cette nouvelle raison nous permet de constater que les faits soidisant connus n'étaient pas aussi connus qu'on croyait. Malgré ça, il arrive que certaines verités de philosophie soient acceptées trop aisement, parce qu'elles expriment des convictions latentes et confuses, ou qu'elles rehaussent des phenomènes familiers. Celui qui n'est pas versé dans les procédés de la recherche phénoménologique peut prendre alors, avec une justification apparente, l'attitude du desabusé. Du même coup, il se montrerait enclin à décompter ces verités, trop aisement acceptées (ce qui est un contresens assez humain). Même l'évidence semble une vulgarité si elle n'offre plus cet élément de surprise, de difficulté, qu'on s'attend à trouver dans les pensées vraiment substantielles de la science.

C'est Nicolai Hartmann, je crois, dans sa *Métaphysique de la Connaissance*, celui qui a mis au jour pour la première fois la structure complexe de ces actes d'identification et d'objectivation. Une double relation avec l'objet serait nécessaire pour obtenir ce qu'il appelle "le critère objectif de verité." L'objectivation n'est possible que parce que chacune des *deux* représentations se rapporte à un *même* terme transcendant, et qu'il y a un accord intérieur entre elles du point de vue de leur contenu. La verité de fait consiste essentiellement dans ce rapport transcendant des deux représentations avec l'objet.

Mais cette dualité (ou pluralité) de représentations implique évidentment un usage spécifique de la mémoire, car il y a un écart temporel entre l'une et l'autre. Le rapport des représentations dans la conscience est condition de possibilité du rapport de ces représentations, dejà ensemblées, à l'objet exterieur. Pourtant, Hartmann ne fait pas une seule fois mention de la mémoire; il laisse sous-entendue sa cooperation dans ce que lui-même juge essentiel dans l'acte de l'objectivation.

Ce n'est pas une donnée négligeable; on ne peut pas dire à son sujet que "cela va de soi." C'est plutôt un supposé qu'on doit faire revenir à la surface. D'abord, parce que la méthode phénoménologique interdit de bâtir sur des supposés; et puis, parce que ce supposé particulier ne vient pas seul, mais fait pendant avec un autre aspect du problème qui reste aussi sous la surface, comme s'il était dejà resolu: celui de la "consistance" ou persistance de l'objet dans cette entité qu'on suppose être *la même* au cours du temps.

II. Une autre façon, dont la vogue se repand de plus en plus, de discréditer une pensée "dejà connue," consiste cette fois à l'attribuer au passé. Cela suffirait à démontrer qu'elle n'est pas vraie, car le passé serait l'archive de toutes les erreurs. Naturellement on ne peut pas faire usage des deux procédés ensemble, ni même successivement: dans un cas, la proposition exprimait une verité trop connue, dans l'autre elle n'exprime qu'une erreur trop ancienne. Donc, selon la logique ancienne, il faudrait se décider pour l'une ou pour l'autre des deux objections.

Il est sans doute possible de relever une certaine ressemblance entre des propositions comme "pas d'identification sans mémoire," "connaître c'est reconnaître," etc. et celle qu'on trouve dans le *Ménon* platonicien: "ce que nous appelons le savoir n'est qu'une réminiscence" (81d). Mais la ressemblance n'est que purement verbale. Encore une fois: de quoi s'agit-il?

D'abord, il s'agit chez Platon d'une espèce de recherche (ξήτησις) tout à fait différente de la recherche phénoménologique. La raison de cette différence est fondamentale. Justement, le problème que Platon se pose est celui de la connaissance d'un être qui n'existe pas dans ce monde, qui n'est pas par consequent visible (il serait ἀειδές). L'être que l'on voit est changeant. La science ne peut se bâtir que sur ce qui persiste sans altération. Donc, cet être qui n'a pas de présence inmédiate, on doit le saisir médiatement. La reminiscence est une sorte de souvenir transcendant, declenché par la vision des objets sensibles.

Il serait gênant d'insister sur la différence entre la mémoire qui participe à l'appréhension des objets sensibles, et la reminiscence d'un être qui par definition est placé hors de la portée des sens. Ce qui devient maintenant nécessaire c'est d'obtenir une compréhension adéquate de la pensée platonicienne. A cause de la nature du problème qu'il examine, ou bien à cause d'une certaine indécision provisoire de sa pensée, Platon fait souvent appel au mythe, à l'allegorie, c'est à dire, à des formes d'exposition que nous jugeons inadmissibles dans notre langage scientifique. Le mythe est une "faveur divine," une inspiration que nous permet de remonter notre condition et de "rendre raison" (λόγον διδόναι) de ce qui se trouve au delà de nos resources mortelles. La reminiscence est mythe et théorie conceptuelle à moitié.

Malgré tout, Platon reussit à se faire comprendre pour n'importe qui se montrerait disposé à la compréhension. Ce qu'il veut dire (et il le dit très bien) c'est qu'il faut établir dans le concept de l'être pur le fondement *a priori* de la connaissance scientifique. Cette thèse est la même que, sous des termes différents, nous retrouvons dans la théorie des idées innées de Descartes, et qui se trouve encore chez Husserl. Quoique nous pouvons nous montrer en désaccord avec l'apriorisme platonicien, son caractère scientifique ne peut pas être mis en doute. Car ce désaccord doit être lui aussi fondé sur des raisons qui touchent au noyau du problème, sur une analyse différente du *factum* de la science. La simple analyse du langage employé par Platon ne serait jamais décisive. En somme, s'il s'agit de savoir comment se forment les principales catégories, et qu'elle est leur valeur, le problème reste sur pied après les analyses linguistiques.

André Mercier

(*Université de Berne*)

DE L'EVIDENCE

Résumé

L'objet de ces lignes est d'expliquer que l'évidence ne doit être cherchée ni dans des prémisses, ni dans des conclusions, qu'elle est absente des mathématiques alors qu'elle ne surgit qu'en rapport avec des situations ontologico-expérientielles. Il y a plusieurs ordres de l'évidence; le plus frappant ressortit à la mystique et le moins manifeste à la démarche objective.

L'évidence est toujours évidence de l'adéquation de la pensée à l'être.

1.1 Rien de moins "évident" que l'évidence elle-même. Leibniz ne voulait-il pas que l'on démontrât ce qui paraît évident?[1] De nos jours d'ailleurs, ne devient-il pas impossible de fonder quoi que ce soit, y compris l'évidence?[2]

1.2 L'anglais dit *obvious*: qui se trouve sous nos pas. Or tout est sous nos pas; il suffit de marcher dessus: *Attamen, cave viperas!*

L'allemand dit *selbstverständlich*: qui se comprend de soi, qui va de soi, ce qui ne veut pas dire grand chose; est-il pensable que quelque chose aille de soi?

Ou alors, n'y a-t-il pas de nombreuses situations qui vont de soi, sans que nous nous en doutions? Et même, toute situation concrète va de soi. Car telle qu'elle est en soi, elle est indubitable. Mais pour qu'elle s'impose telle à l'entendement, elle appelle un effort non seulement de perception (au moins de tourner le regard sur elle) mais aussi un effort de compréhension: com-préhension jusqu'à ce que sa prise soit parfaite, c'est-à-dire que l'image que l'on reconstruit d'elle coïncide avec elle en soi. S'il n'y a pas de situations concrètes en soi,

---

[1] W. Leibniz, *Nouveaux Essais sur l'entendement humain*, Livre IV, Chap. VII. Voir p. ex. au paragraphe 10 (p. 413 des *Sämtl. Schriften*, Bd. 6, Berlin 1962) la citation suivante: Philalethe: "... ces Messieurs, qui prétendent que toute autre connaissance (qui n'est pas de fait) dépend des principes généraux innés et evidens par eux-mêmes..." et la réponse de Theophile.

[2] Cf. les Entretiens d'Aquila de l'I.I.P. (1964) à propos de la mise en question du fondement des droits de l'homme.

n'importe quelle image d'une soi-disant situation peut être déclarée image parfaite; serait-elle pour cela évidente en tant que compréhension de cette situation? Difficilement, car c'est nous-même qui l'aurions "jetée sous nos pas" artificiellement pour marcher dessus, et ce n'est pas ce que le latin *obvius* veut dire. Ne faut-il pas que ce qui est obvius résiste et que nous cessions de résister – nous, et non pas ce que nous rencontrons sous nos pas – pour qu'il y ait évidence?

1.3 Nous savons aujourd'hui qu'on ne peut pas définir les axiomes comme vérités évidentes. Il est douteux qu'il y ait rien d'évident dans l'abstrait. Seul le concret peut aller de soi. Même des principes de la logique sont discutables. Par exemple le tiers n'est plus "évidemment" exclu.

Malheureusement, nous n'avons du concret jamais l'image parfaite: même les théories physiques, si bien adaptées soient-elles aux observations dont elles sont contemporaines, font place à d'autres dites "meilleures," incarnant un plus haut degré de vérité et par conséquent plus efficaces (aussi), si bien que l'évidence du concret semble vaciller à son tour – du moins dans le domaine de la science.

1.4 Qu'en est-il alors des domaines non-scientifiques? Si l'évidence du vrai nous échappe au fur et à mesure que nous le tenons, celle du bien ou celle du beau nous échappent-elles aussi? Il semble que oui: les règles qui fixaient les relations parents-enfants, maître-élève, patron-ouvrier, homme-femme, etc. et qui paraissaient "évidentes" à un âge qu'on pourrait appeler victorien, non seulement font place à d'autres, mais s'évanouissent. Il n'est pas correct de dire qu'elles sont remplacées par des relations objectives, donc de nature scientifique, même si quelquefois la confrontation de l'aspect moral et de l'aspect scientifique contribue à leur disparition, à cause d'un certain déséquilibre qui tend à promouvoir la science bien plus que la morale.[3] L'évidence du beau non plus n'est pas immuable: les styles deviennent peu à peu ennuyeux. Sans cela, pourquoi se succéderaient-ils? Et pourtant, chaque style nouveau enthousiasme la génération montante qui le tient pour expression de ses aspirations.

1.5 On pourrait s'attendre à trouver l'évidence discutée dans les traités sur la théorie de la connaissance. Or il n'en est rien ou presque. Ainsi, V. Kraft[4] ne la discute pas, F. van Steenberghen y consacre[5] quatre ou cinq lignes anodines ...

---

[3] Cf. A. Mercier, *Science and Responsibility* (Torino 1969).

[4] Viktor Kraft, *Erkenntnislehre* (Wien 1960).

[5] F. van Steenberghen, *Erkenntnislehre* (Bd. 2 der Philos. Lovan. Deutsche Ausgabe, Einsiedeln 1950, p. 113).

Quant aux dictionnaires, ils évoquent la certitude, le clair et le distinct cartésiens, l'absence totale du doute, et d'autres notions du même genre. Or de nos jours, la théorie de la science ne fait plus grand place à l'alternative du doute et de la certitude; elle tend vers un probabilisme où l'on attribue aux connaissances partielles des degrés tirés de la probabilité et vers un structuralisme[6] fait de schémas, planning, techniques, feed-back etc. etc.[7]

On imaginerait volontiers un auteur qui déciderait d'éliminer de son vocabulaire les termes de doute, de certitude, et plus particulièrement, d'évidence, parce qu'il les trouverait dépourvus de sens.

1.6 Il y a donc une première éventualité dans laquelle la notion d'évidence se révèle caduque parce que dépourvue de sens dans les conditions actuelles. S'il est impossible de donner à quoi que ce soit un sens "clair et distinct," la théorie de la connaissance ne saurait que faire de la notion d'évidence. L'usage de ce terme se justifierait seulement aux yeux d'un esprit naïf et non-éclairé.

1.7 Mais Descartes était-il naïf et non-éclairé lorsqu'il répétait[8] que c'est par une fiction de l'esprit qu'il commence de douter pour arriver finalement à concevoir clairement et distinctement ... ?

Une question se pose: est-on bien inspiré quand on cherche à caractériser l'évidence en l'opposant au doute?

Car, l'évidence ressortit à ce qui se voit tout à coup, alors qu'on ne l'avait pas vu avant – ce qui n'implique aucune opposition au doute. Ici, le fait que le sens anglais d'*evidence* diffère du français ou de l'allemand nous éclaire un peu mieux. Cette différence a été relevée notamment par Bertrand Russell.[9] En anglais, le vocable peut se mettre facilement au pluriel, au sens de constats; p. ex. des constats policiers. Il s'enrichit alors d'une plus grande réalité. C'est là, d'ailleurs, un exemple de la différence systématique entre la langue anglaise et les langues européennes continentales: L'anglais tend à ne s'appliquer jamais qu'à des cas d'espèces; toute la philosophie d'un B. Russell est bâtie sur un enchaînement de cas d'espèce (surtout dans ses conférences). Les langues continentales tendent par contre à abstraire et à susciter des sens génériques aux mots. Cette différence est le plus claire, dans le cadre de la philosophie, à propos du substantif *être*. Il n'y a pour l'anglais que des *beings*, *des* êtres, en alle-

---

[6] A ne pas confondre avec le structuralisme philosophique (Levi-Strauss etc.).

[7] Voir p. ex. les Rapports "On Complex Systems," contributions de H. Törnebohm et al. (*Planification du Ministère de la Défense nationale*, Stockholm 1968).

[8] Dans la Réponse aux Secondes Objections (aux Méditations) recueillies par Mersenne.

[9] Note au Vocab. de la Philosophie de Lalande (4ème éd. Paris 1938, Vol. I, p. 224).

mand *Seiende,* il n'y a pas l'être au singulier, que même le mot de
reality ne rend pas (tout au plus le *really real* de B. Russell). En revanche, l'ontologie continentale n'hésite pas à utiliser le vocable, au
singulier, pour dire par exemple de lui[10] qu'il est "la première
évidence" et la "source de toutes les autres évidences." Ainsi
Gabriel Marcel[11] parle de l'être[12] et Heidegger évoque "das Sein."[13]

2. De ces quelques remarques, nous tirons une leçon: L'évidence a
peut-être quand même un sens. Mais 1° elle n'est en aucun cas l'affaire
de la logique, 2° elle est toujours l'affaire de l'ontologie. Si donc la
théorie de la connaissance compte lui réserver une place, ce sera la
théorie d'une connaissance ontologique et non pas une psychologie.

Précisions que, si la philosophie continentale considère la notion
d'évidence comme enracinée dans l'être primordial indifférencié aussi
bien que dans les divers êtres différenciés, la philosophie anglaise[14]
(mais non pas nécessairement américaine), ne s'attache qu'aux êtres
dans les diverses situations où on les rencontre. L'*obvious* est alors
effectivement ce que l'on reconnait comme indubitable "sur son
chemin"; mais ces évidences-constats ne sont pas celles qui intéres-
sent la théorie de la connaissance, elles sont des faits (cf. plus loins
à propos de l'histoire).

En effet, aucune théorie n'opère avec des cas d'espèces. II n'y a
théorie que lorsque, à partir des cas d'espèces, on abstrait les
généralités ayant caractère d'universaux. Sinon, on reste dans l'histoire au sens de la chronique. Le sens, que l'on peut appeler "anglais,"
des mots – que ce soit ici du mot être ou du mot évidence – rend une
théorie de la connaissance quasi impossible, à moins de confondre
cette théorie avec l'élaboration pure et simple de la logique étrangère,
elle, à l'ontologie; mais alors, notre problème serait un faux problème,

[10] F. van Steenberghen, *Ontologie* (*ibid.* Bd. 4, p. 62).
[11] G. Marcel: *Etre et Avoir* (Paris, 1935).
[12] Avec une certaine inquiétude! (Remarque de M. Gabriel Marcel lui-même qui a eu
la gentillesse de prendre connaissance du présent exposé et en a approuvé la teneur.)
[13] Faut il, nous a demandé Monsieur Ricœur –, renoncer à tout ce qui est impliqué
par les diverses métaphores de la vision qui désignent l'intuition? A cette question nous
répondons que l'intuition est distincte de l'évidence; elle est bien plus au début d'un
processus d'approche de la compréhension de l'être qu'à son issue où l'éclair de l'évidence
a lieu (voir plus loin).
Faut-il, – continue-t-il, – renoncer à ce qui est impliqué par les métaphores de la con-
trainte, de la résistance à l'arbitraire (quand on dit p. ex.: c'est ainsi, car je le vois, – car
je ne puis autrement...)? La réponse à cette question est donnée par la définition de la
réalité comme ce qui résiste et par la remarque que l'évidence est, de la part du sujet, un
renoncement à la résistance qu'il aurait, lui, tendance à opposer à la compréhension des
choses (cf. 1.2 ad finem).
[14] A quelques exceptions près. Cf. par exemple Agnes Arber, *The Manifold and the One*
(London 1957), où l'évidence d'ordre mystique est rendue à l'aide du vocable d'*awareness.*

puisqu'il n'y a pas d'évidence en logique. La tendance, manifeste de quelques écoles anglo-saxonnes, de faire quand même de l'ontologie avec des espèces d'êtres de raison (de raison mathématico-logique) est totalement étrangère aux préoccupations d'un savant positif, dont le métier est de faire de la physique; ce genre d'ontologie est, pour lui, "vide" de contenu existentiel,[15] elle ne traite de rien du tout au sens qu'elle ignore s'il y a une réalité à laquelle les constructions de l'esprit s'appliquent.

3.1 Nous retournerons donc à une théorie de la connaissance suffisamment imprégnée d'ontologie véritable pour nous permettre d'affirmer: *La notion d'évidence n'a de sens qu'en rapport avec l'expérience que l'on a de l'être ou des êtres.*

Mais l'expérience ne doit aucunement être identifiée à l'expérience objective seulement. Les expériences objectives ne forment qu'un sous-ensemble des expériences possibles.

Schématiquement toute expérience se scinde en trois moments: a) La préparation. Il peut s'agir d'expérience scientifique préparée, ou *experiment,* pour utiliser le terme anglais ou allemand. Elle est préparée par le sujet pensant ou agissant; c'est le sens généralement réservé au mot *experiment*; mais elle peut aussi "se trouver préparée" par le concours de circonstances qui mettent le sujet en présence de la situation toute prête, et l'obligent à concentrer son attention sur le cas d'espèce comme il le fait volontairement dans l'experiment. Il n'y a pas lieu de faire de différence pour notre argument. Il peut s'agir aussi de la préparation (voulue ou suscitée par les circonstances) à l'engagement de l'artiste dans la création d'une oeuvre, ou à l'engagement d'un sujet en présence d'autres sujets avec qui il entretient des relations morales, ou encore à la communion supraphénoménale de l'union mystique avec l'être. De nouveau, nous n'avons ici pas besoin de distinguer tous ces cas. Ils relèvent tous de ce que nous appellerons "l'expérience circonstancielle."

Au premier moment de l'élaboration de l'expérience circonstancielle se superpose un second que voici: (b) Le sujet prend conscience de la relation qui lie une réponse particulière à une question particulière impliquée toutes deux par la préparation de l'expérience circonstancielle.[16] Un effort de pensée s'avère alors nécessaire pour

---

[15] Cf. d'ailleurs B. Russell, Introduction à la philosophie mathématique: "... aucun principe de logique ne peut assurer 'l'existence' ...." (Trad. française, Paris 1928, p. 242).

[16] Dans le cas de l'expérience mystique, le mot de particulière doit être remplacé par celui d'unique au sens impliqué p. ex. par l'invocation qui ouvre le Vicharasangraham de Bhagavan Sri Ramana Maharshi (voir la Trad. anglaise de T. M. P. Mahadevan, 7e éd., Tiruvannamalai 1965: "Is there any way ..., except by abiding ...").

adapter la question et la réponse l'une à l'autre jusqu'à ce qu'elles s'harmonisent réalisant alors deux conditions : (i) le sujet est certain de posséder la réponse correcte à une question correctement posée ; (ii) le sujet est certain de pouvoir communiquer, et la question et la réponse, à d'autres sujets susceptibles de faire à leur tour, avec une approximation suffisante, la même expérience circonstancielle pour en tirer, avec une même approximation, le même couple question-réponse.[17]

La première de ces conditions est plus facile à réaliser que la seconde. D'une part, celle-ci n'est jamais qu'approximativement réalisée (ne serait-ce qu'à cause du πάντα ρει héraclitéen, mais plus encore parce que la communication d'un résultat quelconque obtenu par un premier sujet ajoute les circonstances de cette communication à celles de l'expérience circonstancielle d'autres sujets sous la forme d'un préjugé dont on ne peut se débarasser totalement ; ainsi il est faux de prétendre qu'en science nous puissions répéter exactement les vérifications expérimentales, car nous les changeons toujours dans la pratique). Ensuite, de toute expérience circonstantielle ressort un couple question-réponse impliquant une spécialité quelconque (la physique, la biologie, . . . ou la musique, la sculpture, etc.). Aussi vaste que son champ puisse être, celle-ci requiert du sujet qui réalise ou reproduit (approximativement) l'expérience non seulement un talent spécial mais encore l'éducation nécessaire dans cette spécialité.

c) A ces deux moments succède un troisième qui, au contraire des deux premiers, n'a pas le caractère de phases, mais celui d'un éclair : La prise de conscience finale, subite et sans durée, foudroyante (au figuré), de ce que le couple formé de la réponse et de la question recouvre sans faille visible une réalité ontique ; en d'autres termes, c'est la certitude immédiate[18] que la bonne question a été posée à propos d'une réalité justement circonstanciée et que la réponse y est trouvée. Cet éclair est un enrichissement de la pensée ; c'est lui qu'il faut appeler l'évidence ; et puisque, de l'avis de tout le monde, un enrichissement entraîne un surcroît de valeur, *l'évidence est donc l'évidence d'une valeur.*[19] La valeur, sans être matérielle comme une pièce d'or, un kilogramme de denrée, un hectare de terrain, . . . peut se

---

[17] Nous sommes contraints d'employer, malgré ce qui a été dit plus haut, le vocable de certain. Mais l'indubitable qui y ressortit n'a de sens qu'après l'éclair de l'évidence (voir (c) ci-dessous).

[18] C'est-à-dire sans plus aucun intermédiaire, où les "illusions de l'immédiat" dont parle Hegel et sur lesquelles M. Ricœur a attiré notre attention ne nous concernent plus, parce que, ensuite de cet immédiat de l'évidence, la dialectique s'effondre et l'écart initial entre l'immédiat et le dire de l'immédiat disparaît.

[19] Dans l'ouvrage *Thought and Being* (Bâle 1959), nous avons expliqué que la valeur est de nature empirique.

transmettre de sujet à sujet et se reconnaître comme telle, identique à elle-même en tant qu'en soi et comparable à elle-même dans les conceptions qu'en ont les sujets individuels suffisamment bons spécialistes pour s'entendre sur elle sans dispute. Quelquefois, on lui attribue un nombre (un prix), mais ce n'est que pour faciliter le commerce.[20]

3.2 Telle est la seconde conclusion à laquelle nous parvenons. Elle n'identifie pas l'évidence à l'expérience, mais place l'évidence à l'issue foudroyante qui suit les phases de l'expérience. En particulier, le caractère de fulguration n'est pas celui de l'expérience, mais celui de l'évidence.

Mais cette conclusion est entachée de la double approximation provenant de l'imprécision circonstancielle et des différences entre les sujets qui se la communiquent.

C'est pourquoi l'évidence conserve toujours une appréciation individuelle qui fait dire : "ceci ou cela m'est (personnellement) évident dans les circonstances présentes," ou encore: "telle et telle est la valeur que je puis attribuer à ces choses." L'évidence n'apparaît qu'au terme d'un chemin parcouru individuellement,[21] terme clair et distinct, perçu en un éclair dans une vision véritable, authentique et obligatoire.

Pour le premier sujet qui discerne une nouvelle évidence, le chemin peut avoir été long et ardu. En revanche, pour les autres sujets qui en prennent connaissance à leur tour, ce chemin est souvent fort raccourci, réduit quelquefois à presque rien (à condition toutefois qu'ils soient suffisamment bons spécialistes): la simple exposition de la réponse à la question suffit à faire éclore l'être auquel il s'applique. C'est alors l'évidence au sens commun.

4.1 Or, les valeurs se classent selon des ordres; donc il y a des ordres d'évidence correspondants. Puisque l'évidence ressortit à l'expérience, on reconnaîtra ces ordres à partir des divers ordres expérientiels auxquels nous avons fait allusion plus haut. L'évidence étant l'aboutissement qui ne laisse, de la démarche expérientielle, plus régner de

---

[20] La douleur qu'on ressent si un objet lourd échappé de notre main nous tombe sur le pied p. ex., n'est pas en soi une expérience. Elle ne fait partie d'une expérience que si l'on élabore un système qui englobe le problème qu'elle pose, la réponse à ce problème et les circonstances auxquelles ce problème se rattache: p. ex. une théorie de la gravitation ajoutée à celle du choc ou p. ex. un exercice de discipline morale qui transfigure la douleur en une acceptation de notre maladresse, etc.

[21] P. W. Bridgman (Prix Nobel) a beaucoup insisté sur la nécessité de ce cheminement individuel. Cf. p. ex. son ouvrage *Reflections of a Physicist* (2nd ed. New York 1955), spéc. p. 46 ss.

perplexité et qui détruit la phase inquiète pour la remplacer par une phase positive des démarches cognitives, nous pourrions nous demander tout d'abord quel est l'ordre des expériences les plus foudroyantes dans leur positivité, celles qui non seulement ne laissent plus aucune hésitation, mais qui n'en ont peut-être jamais laissé régner aucune du moment où elles ont été circonstanciées. Pour ne pas faire un jeu de mot, nous ne dirons pas que la réponse à cette question est "évidente," mais en la donnant, nous croyons qu'elle le deviendra au sens naïf du terme: ce sont les expériences mystiques. L'expérience mystique est, d'ailleurs la plus positive de toutes les expériences parce qu'elle est ontique[22] par excellence; en elle, les circonstances englobent toujours l'être dans sa totalité,[23] mais le jugement sur l'objet par le sujet fait place au rapport inverse où c'est le sujet qui est "jugé" par l'être.

Or l'expérience mystique, pour positive qu'elle soit, n'est ni objective, ni subjective, ni morale.[24] Sa nature est telle que l'être du sujet y reflète la totalité de l'être qui est plus que la somme des êtres, raison pour laquelle elle est la moins communicable, bien que tous les mystiques – ces spécialistes de l'expérience ontique – soient en meilleur accord que tous les savants d'une même branche, parce qu'ils s'entendent non seulement entre contemporains d'un même niveau d'instruction dans un même domaine, mais à travers le temps et l'espace géographique. L'expérience ontique du mystique n'est d'ailleurs jamais circonstanciée de la même façon que les autres, puisqu'elle est la seule qui se passe de limites. En même temps, elle aboutit à la plus grande évidence, disons même à la seule évidence qui mérite sans restriction ce nom et qui satisfasse sans ambages à la première partie de la définition de van Steenberghen dans son Ontologie.[25]

Mais un grand nombre d'individus ne sont pas mystiques, n'étant spécialistes que de tel ou tel domaine soumis à des bornes qu'ils ne transcendent que par un effort métaphysique qui reste étranger à l'évidence de l'expérience ontique globale.

4.2 Il y a d'abord les artistes. Par là, nous entendons en premier lieu

[22] Ontique: de l'être, ou des êtres. Ontologique: de la théorie (ou d'une théorie) de l'être ou des êtres. (Ces sens diffèrent de ceux utilisés par Heidegger).

[23] Toutes les autres expériences n'atteignent l'être que dans ses particularités.

[24] La distinction de ces quatre ordres a été faite dans plusieurs de nos ouvrages. Voir p. ex. *Erkenntnis und Wirklichkeit* (Bern und München 1968), ou la première contribution aux Entretiens d'Oberhofen de l'I.I.P. (Actes publiés dans Dialectica, 57/58, Vol. 15, pp. 1–336, Neuchâtel 1961).

[25] F. van Steenberghen, *Ontologie* (*loc. cit.*). En font preuve tous les mystiques jusqu'aux contemporains tels que L. Wittgenstein, ou Simone Weil.

les créateurs parmi eux. Leur œuvre entière est une suite d'expériences circonstancielles destinées à faire surgir l'évidence de la beauté qui est le garant que l'œuvre est la réponse convenant à une question bien posée à la réalité. Toute œuvre artistique que son auteur a finalement livrée au public est censée porter le signe de l'affirmation qu'il a abouti à une évidence. Ce signe est extrêmement concret, puisqu'il est fait de pierre, de pâtes de couleur sur la toile, de sons reproductibles par les voix humaines ou instrumentales, etc. Il est perceptible pour chacun,[26] bien que "recopier les œuvres" ou s'en inspirer aveuglement soit tenu tout au plus pour un exercice utile, sinon pour un plagiat et que, par conséquent, la reproduction de l'expérience circonstancielle ne soit pas "bien vue." Mais l'évidence du beau qui jaillit d'une œuvre d'art se communique très vite, c'est-à-dire sans l'intermédiaire d'une longue reproduction expérientielle à tous ceux qui ont assez de talent et d'exercice pour la saisir. L'interprétation dans l'exécution musicale, théâtrale et chorégraphique se prêterait à une analyse détaillée utile à la compréhension de la notion d'expérience circonstancielle. Nous n'entreprendrons pas une telle analyse ici; signalons seulement que les chefs d'orchestre et les exécutants sont les plus aptes à établir que le beau relève d'évidences universellement reconnaissables; cela s'explique par la publicité qu'ils leur donnent au travers des œuvres qu'ils interprètent. (On notera aussi les différences d'interprétations, qui marquent l'approximation dont il a été question plus haut.) Mais la communication d'évidence ainsi réalisée intervient au terme d'une approche proprement artistique qui fait refaire le chemin de pénétration selon le mode d'un jugement nécessairement subjectif sans lequel rien d'artistique n'est promu. Ce qui n'empêche pas que l'évidence du beau s'impose comme épreuve authentique d'un aspect de l'être ou des êtres. Les vrais artistes s'accordent tous à dire que leurs œuvres sont des représentations authentiques de la réalité, et s'il y a des philosophes pour dire que l'art n'est que fantaisie parce que subjectif, ces philosophes sont des ignorants, c'est-à-dire des non-spécialistes à qui manquent et le talent de création ou d'appréciation, et l'exercice de l'art jusqu'aux exécutions difficiles des œuvres contemporaines, ce qui leur défend d'en parler en connaissance de cause, tout comme ils ne sauraient parler d'une science qu'ils n'auraient pas apprise et cultivée eux-mêmes.[26a]

---

[26] Aveugles, sourds ... exceptés.

[26a] La beauté d'un paysage ne s'impose qu'à la suite d'une éducation (plus ou moins naturelle) qui fait de chaque amateur de la nature un spécialiste. A leur tour, un géographe ou un peintre en donneront chacun l'évidence qu'ils ont trouvées par l'exercice de leur profession.

Il est d'ailleurs maladroit de classer, comme on le fait quelquefois, les approches de l'être en objectives et non-objectives. Car l'objectivité n'est pas le critère de l'authenticité de la promotion des valeurs. L'objectivité n'est qu'un mode, efficace, parmi d'autres. La subjectivité en est un autre. L'évidence du beau est, après celle – mystique – de la totalité de l'être, la plus forte en ce qu'elle laisse le mieux s'éffrondrer le doute sur l'adéquation de l'appréhension des choses par l'intellect.[27] En effet, l'appréhension artistique met l'intellect en contact particulièrement intime avec ces choses (au contraire du mode objectif) – contact dont on ne peut bien entendu pas dire qu'il soit physique, mais dont il faut reconnaître qu'il exige une subordination du sujet qui est le caractère même de la subjectivité.

4.3 Kant a analysé avec beaucoup de clarté la forme morale de l'évidence pour en faire une catégorie importante, dans la notion de l'impératif.[28] On peut, et l'on doit même identifier avec une évidence du bien chaque maxime qui satisfait à l'impératif catégorique kantien. Mais l'ordre de connaissance auquel il correspond n'est plus ici ni ontique, ni subjectif, ni objectif; il est, à proprement parler, social[29] ou communautaire, car l'impératif moral requiert une action impliquant harmonieusement les divers membres d'une communauté ou d'une société.

Nombre d'auteurs n'auraient pas pensé qu'il fût utile, voir désirable de mettre la notion d'évidence en relation avec une autre démarche que l'objective. A peu près les mêmes auteurs auraient estimé qu'il n'y pas de connaissance en dehors d'une démarche objective. Mais cette double opinion est loin d'être acceptée par tout le monde, car elle ne résiste pas à la critique, parce qu'elle invoque toujours mais à tort la prétention que seule le démarche objective accède à l'accord universel, ce qui est doublement faux car, 1° il n'est jamais possible d'accéder à un accord véritablement universel et, 2°, l'accord des esprits se fait tout aussi bien le long de voies non-objectives (toujours entre spécialistes, comme c'est le cas pour la démarche objective; les spécialistes ne constituent jamais l'universalité du genre humain).

Mais d'autre part, il faut reconnaître qu'àu travers des décennies, peut-être même des siècles de pensée théorique, l'idée d'évidence, pour autant qu'elle est venue aux penseurs, est venue en rapport

---

[27] Se rappeler la définition thomiste – toujours valable – de la connaissance par l'*adaequatio*.

[28] Sans le caractériser cependant comme évidence parce qu'il ne s'est pas aperçu que c'en était une.

[29] A ne pas confondre avec sociologique.

avec la connaissance objective de la vérité plutôt qu'en rapport avec
celle, subjective, de l'art, celle, communautaire de la morale, ou celle,
ontique de la mystique. C'est pourquoi, quittant ici l'impératif
moral, nous passerons à une analyse un peu plus longue de l'évidence
objective.

4.4 Nous avons déjà relevé que, de nos jours, on ne peut plus invo-
quer l'évidence pour énoncer un axiome. Mais la question se pose de
savoir si l'on peut parler d'évidence à l'autre extrémité du raisonne-
ment mathématique, c'est-à-dire au terme de la démonstration.
Ainsi, une fois comprise p. ex. la démonstration du théorème de
Pythagore, le contenu de ce théorème est-il évident? Il n'est pas si
simple de répondre. Il n'y a pas de triangles euclidiens concrets. Il
n'y a que l'idée d'un tel triangle, c'est un être de raison. Donc la
question s'étend aux êtres de raison: leurs propriétés, une fois re-
connues, sont-elles évidentes? Je veux bien concéder qu'on parle
ainsi et qu'on dise oui, mais je préférerais de beaucoup que l'on refuse
aux êtres de raison l'évidence afin de ne pas tomber dans la confusion
du tautologique et du non-tautologique. En outre, il y a une raison
plus profonde à refuser l'évidence au contenu des théorèmes démon-
trés; c'est que la mathématique n'a pas la nature d'un savoir, mais
celle d'un pouvoir. C'est pourquoi ses opérations et ses enchaînements
ne sont jamais *vrais* au sens où on peut les trouver réalisés dans l'être
concret et historique, ils sont *justes*, c'est-à-dire construits de manière
à éviter la contradiction. La non-contradiction ne définit pas la
vérité.

Nous ne traiterons pas ici du mystère de l'efficacité des mathématiques dans l'analyse de la réalité concrète. Nous dirons simplement que la notion d'évidence devrait être bannie du domaine des
mathématiques pures. Il n'est pas "évident" du tout que $2 \times 4 =$
$= 4 \times 2$, que $a \times b = b \times a$; il n'y a aucun impératif pour cela.
Deux fois quatre pommes et quatre fois deux pommes sont des semi-
phrases insuffisantes pour être comparées. Pourquoi des pommes,
d'ailleurs, s'il s'agit de mathématiques pures? La théorie des quanta
travaille avec une algèbre où $a \times b$ peut différer de $b \times a$. La
physique moderne a réduit à néant toute évidence dite mathématique en montrant qu'il faut construire une mathématique adaptée
à chaque catégorie de problèmes physiques; c'est une part de l'ap-
prêtage des expériences circonstancielles des physiciens, mais ce
n'est pas le moment que nous appelons l'évidence.

4.5 Si l'évidence n'a pas de sens pour la mathématique, en a-t-elle un du côté opposé de la démarche objective de l'esprit humain? D'abord, quel est cet autre côté? C'est l'histoire: non pas au sens spécial de l'herméneutique mais l'histoire (toute simple) des hommes et des choses. Dans ce sens, en effet, si la mathématique a toujours affaire aux universaux, ce n'est jamais le cas de l'histoire; elle ne s'attache qu'à préciser et ordonner des situations particulières et uniques: les faits ou particularités (en anglais selon le langage des logisticiens: *particulars*). Mais l'historicité des faits ou *particulars* n'est à son tour pas plus la vérité que la justesse des procédés mathématiques. Un fait particulier n'est jamais vrai en soi, il n'a aucune valeur qui puisse se transmettre. Il ne faut pas dire: "il est vrai que Napoléon . . ."; il faut dire: "c'est un fait que Napoléon . . ." ou "il est historique que Napoléon . . ."[29a] L'absence de la vérité des faits historiques devient claire aussitôt qu'on remarque l'impossibilité de les appréhender par une expérience circonstancielle. Une expérience circonstancielle devient un fait historique, mais elle n'est pas à son tour expérienciable. Il n'y a donc pas d'évidence attachée à l'histoire – et, d'ailleurs, pour la même raison, l'histoire n'est pas une science, bien qu'elle soit nécessaire à la science.

4.6 Une science[30] est quelque compromis de mathématique et d'histoire, car elle consiste toujours à établir la validité d'universaux parmi les particularités historiques (les *particulars*). Ce n'est qu'une fois cet établissement amorcé que des vérités surgissent et s'emboîtent et que l'on peut parler de valeur. Alors les vérités se transmettent comme il se doit de toute valeur. L'évidence y trouve place, car en elle réside le critère de l'adéquation de l'abstrait au concret, de la théorie à la praxis. Elle est le signe-éclair que l'union réalisée du mathématique et de l'historique n'est ni une vulgaire juxtaposition de deux choses, ni une trivialité, mais qu'elle constitue structurellement un recouvrement harmonieux de la réalité.[31]

Toutefois, ce que nous avons dit de son surgissement à l'issue de l'expérience circonstancielle est insuffisant. D'une part, une seule expérience n'est qu'un maillon dans une longue chaîne. De l'autre, toute expérience circonstancielle est précédée d'un préjugé utilisé à titre de pré-évidence qui s'affirmera soit comme mal, soit comme bien-jugé. C'est pourquoi l'évidence est un aboutissement. Chez le premier esprit parvenu à elle, elle couronne un effort soutenu vers

---

[29a] Ou mieux encore: "Napoléon . . ."

[30] Par science, donc, nous entendons toujours une science positive; mais c'est alors un pléonasme que de la spécifier comme positive.

[31] Sur le sens de ce recouvrement, voir notre ouvrage: *Erkenntnis und Wirklichkeit* (*loc. cit.*).

une compréhension plus vraie de la réalité. Chez les auditeurs de ce premier, elle est le critère d'un acquiescement qui rend la compréhension publique.

A l'opposé de l'évidence mystique, l'évidence objective est la moins frappante de toutes, parce qu'elle engage le moins le sujet. En d'autres termes, dans la démarche objective, le sujet garde envers l'évidence une sérénité qui ressemble à la passivité quand on la compare à celles des autres ordres. En science, ce qui est devenu évident est immédiatement classique. Mais ce qui est classique doit être dépassé, sinon il n'y aurait plus de recherche scientifique. L'évidence est évidence par rapport à l'ensemble des suppositions faites: adoption des règles d'une logique, choix des axiomes d'une théorie mathématique en application, postulats nécessaires à une dynamique adaptée, lois de la nature valables à la lumière de cette dynamique, conditions initiales et aux limites, simplifications ou approximations faites pour bien poser et résoudre le problème – ceci dans le cas d'une démarche en physique.

Il faut se garder d'un langage propre aux gens non prévenus. Il est fréquent d'entendre quelqu'un s'exclamer: "Cela est évident!" Les mêmes gens s'exclament aussi: "C'est logique!" etc. Ce sont des façons grossières et schématiques d'exprimer qu'une formule leur est familière, ou qu'un enchaînement leur paraît nécessaire. Mais l'enchaînement ne ressortit souvent pas à la logique, ou la formule est éventuellement mensongère. Assez souvent, l'évidence intervient lorsqu'un interlocuteur s'aperçoit qu'il fallait énoncer une supposition ignorée jusqu'ici pour qu'une conclusion s'applique bien à une situation réelle; on dira p. ex.: "Ce n'est que si ..., qu'alors ...," évoquant par là des cas contraires susceptibles d'infirmer la conclusion et obligeant à se concentrer sur un problème correctement circonstancié par les restrictions faites.

4.7 Revenons alors à l'évidence de la beauté pour faire, par comparaison, ressortir un caractère qui ne se rencontre guère que dans l'évidence objective. Lorsqu'un artiste achève une œuvre d'art, celle-ci est presque toujours d'une très grande complexité. L'auteur du buste d'Einstein exposé dans la bibliothèque de l'Institut de Princeton, p. ex., tout en se référant principalement aux yeux et à la chevelure bien connus de l'original, ne précise nulle part, dans un traité ou dans un commentaire, les présupposés de l'œuvre. Si, dans une théorie physique, l'ensemble des règles mathématiques précède l'élaboration finale, dans l'élaboration d'une œuvre artistique en revanche l'esthétique se précise au fur et à mesure. (On peut expliquer cette différence par l'opposition de l'objectif et du subjectif.) Dans la contemplation esthétique, on peut se passer de préciser ces présupposés, car justement ils apparaissent *post opus*; l'évidence est à la disposition du sujet qui s'en empare comme valeur de beauté, car elle est attachée à l'oeuvre en tant qu'elle est la réponse, seule importante, à un problème devenu inutile et qu'on oublie. Au terme d'une démarche objective, le rapport est inversé: l'évidence est attachée bien plus au problème qu'à la réponse: Ce qu'une théorie précise, c'est le problème qu'elle permet de résoudre; la réponse peut s'oublier.[32] Mais alors l'évidence n'est pas au même titre à la disposition du sujet, qui ne peut pas s'en emparer, car on s'empare des réponses pour les colporter, mais non des problèmes; bien plus: ce sont ici les problèmes qui s'emparent de vous (tout cela au figuré). Alors, l'évidence étant essentiellement l'évidence du problème, la démarche objective nous enseigne quels sont les problèmes (les vrais problèmes), en les énonçant; c'est en cela que réside la connaissance de la vérité, et c'est la raison qui fait dire à beaucoup de penseurs que la vérité n'est pas une valeur.[33]

Aussi longtemps qu'on n'en a pas l'évidence objective, un soit-disant problème – vraisemblablement mal posé d'ailleurs – risque toujours encore d'être un pseudo-problème. C'est en particulier le grand danger de la métaphysique, cette démarche objective qui aimerait s'attaquer à l'être pour en connaître la réalité ontique et totale: la métaphysique offre si peu d'évidences![34]

5. Conclusions. L'évidence est un moment essentiel de toute connaissance, car elle en fournit la garantie. La garantie de la connaissance ne réside pas dans une "vérification";[35] la vérification est un mot pour un ensemble de procédés.

Mais toute garantie peut devenir caduque et l'évidence s'évanouir. C'est notamment le cas chaque fois que des conditions nouvelles font sauter la fermeture des expériences circonstancielles tenues (provisoirement) pour closes; ce phénomène de réouverture s'observe dans tous les ordres même mystique.[36]

---

[32] La réponse y est d'ailleurs de nature plus expérimentale, le problème de nature plus théorique. Et il est bien vrai que les traités de physique – pour prendre l'exemple de la science la plus évoluée – ne sont en somme jamais que les exposés de théories admises, c'est-à-dire des problèmes que l'on sait correctement poser.

[33] Lavelle, par exemple.

[34] Ne pas confondre la métaphysique avec la mystique, cette dernière, au contraire de la première, n'étant pas une démarche objective. Voir A Mercier, *Thought and Being* (*loc. cit.*, spéc. p. 139).

[35] Avec les réserves bien connues dues à K. Popper.

[36] Ce phénomène n'est pas étranger à ce qui engage à suivre F. Gonseth dans sa doctrine d'une "philosophie ouverte."

Si la tradition d'une conception naïve pouvait faire croire au 17e siècle que l'évidence est ce qui sert d'indicateur dans le choix des maximes et autres sortes de prémisses, aujourd'hui cette opinion a perdu tout crédit. Cela ne veut pas dire qu'on doive chercher l'évidence dans les conclusions: toute conclusion obtenue par voie reconnue valide à partir des prémisses s'impose si les prémisses sont déjà acceptées, il n'y a donc pas besoin d'y ajouter l'évidence.

Par contre, l'évidence est nécessaire pour justifier la prétention que le cheminement de la pensée, de l'action, de la création, de la contemplation ... est adéquat à la réalité. Lorsque cette adéquation a lieu, il faut nécessairement que l'on trouve la réalité au cours de ce cheminement: *ob-vius*, d'où l'évidence, *obviousness* en anglais, au moment où cette adéquation se manifeste.

G. H. von Wright

(Academy of Finland)

WITTGENSTEIN ON CERTAINTY

1. During the last year and a half of his life Wittgenstein wrote almost exclusively about knowledge and certainty, commenting on some of G. E. Moore's views.[1] These writings were published 1969 under the title *Über Gewissheit – On Certainty*. They possess a thematic unity which makes them almost unique in Wittgenstein's whole literary output. One can speculate about the reasons for this. Does it signalize a change in Wittgenstein's philosophic style? Or does it only show that the author was loosing his power of keeping a thousand threads of thought in his hand at once? There is no indication, however, that the quality of the thoughts is declining. Considering that the remarks constitute a first, unrevised manuscript they seem to me remarkably accomplished both in form and content.

Wittgenstein's treatise on certainty can be said to summarize some of the essential novelties of his thinking. But it does this in a way which is rather different from any which, to the best of my knowledge, Wittgenstein's numerous commentators have tried. The book opens new vistas on his philosophic achievement. Since Wittgenstein's literally last work cannot (yet) be assumed to be widely known even inside the philosophic community, I shall here try to give a brief presentation of its main ideas. I shall not make any attempt to evaluate it critically – nor try to indicate the extent to which I can agree myself with what Wittgenstein has to say. But I shall at the end sketch a few of its implications, as I see them, for further research.

2. A main problem of epistemology since Descartes has been whether any single contingent proposition can be known for certain to be

---

[1] See the editors' Preface to Ludwig Wittgenstein, *Über Gewissheit* (Basil Blackwell, Oxford, 1969). See also the brief but excellent account of conversations with Wittgenstein in the summer of 1949 in Norman Malcolm, *Ludwig Wittgenstein, A Memoir* (Oxford University Press, 1958), pp. 87–92.

true. Moore claimed that *he knew* a great number of such propositions. He gave as examples, among others, that he was a human being, that the object he was now pointing to was his hand, or that the earth has existed for many years past. Since he knew such things, he could also prove that there existed a world external to his mind – and thereby settle, so he thought, a problem long under dispute. Moore further claimed that such items as those just mentioned were by no means known exclusively to him, but that they were specimens of what most human beings under normal circumstances can rightly claim to know.

Moore thought, moreover, that our knowledge of most of these "common sense" propositions, as he called them, is founded on some *evidence* for their truth.[2] But which this evidence is we often cannot tell. We are all, Moore said, "in this strange position that we do *know* many things, with regard to which we *know* further that we must have had evidence for them, and yet we do not know *how* we know them, *i.e.* we do not know what the evidence was."[3]

In order to appreciate both Moore's position and Wittgenstein's criticism of it, it is important to keep the distinction clear between the "common sense" propositions which Moore claimed he knew and the philosophical propositions which he thought provable[4] on their basis. Moore thought of the members of both classes of propositions as being *contingent* truths.[5] This opinion may seem very natural as far as the various propositions of the first category are concerned. With regard to the propositions of the second category this view seems much less natural or even quite dubious. Yet Moore was of the opinion that it is a contingent truth that there is an external world, that time is real, or that there exist selves. To deny these things is not

---

[2] "A Defense of Common Sense," p. 44. References are to G. E. Moore, *Philosophical Papers* (Allen & Unwin, London, 1959).

[3] *Ib.*

[4] The idea of a proof does not appear until the paper "Proof of an External World." But it is implicit already in "A Defence of Common Sense." The known "common sense" propositions *imply*, Moore says there (p. 38), the reality of material things, *etc.*

[5] Neither in "A Defense of Common Sense " nor in "Proof of an External World" does Moore use the term "contingent (proposition)." In the first paper he says (p. 42) that "it seems to me quite clear that it *might* have been the case that Time was not real, material things not real, Space not real, selves not real." In his later paper called "Certainty," however, Moore employs the term "contingent proposition" for "proposition which is not self-contradictory and of which the contradictory is not self-contradictory" (*Philosophical Papers*, p. 230). He also says that "from the fact that a given proposition might have been true it always follows that the proposition in question is not self-contradictory" (*ib.*). From this we can conclude that, according to Moore, a proposition affirming or denying the reality of time or of material things is contingent. But Moore also says that propositions which he thinks he knows for certain such as that he is now standing up, are contingent. (*Ib.*). It is therefore safe to attribute to Moore the view that propositions of both the classes which we have here distinguished are contingent.

to maintain anything which is logically impossible, *i.e.* self-contradictory.

Suppose somebody wanted to dispute some of the things Moore
claimed to know for certain, *e.g.* that he, Moore, was a human being
or was pointing now to his right hand. This critic would then have
to adduce some evidence showing that Moore was mistaken. Moore
again would have to accept this evidence, if he was going to give up
his claim to knowledge. But what could this evidence be, other than
some contingent propositions which contradicted the first ones and
which Moore, "on second thoughts," would have to admit as true?
And then it would still be the case that there existed a great many
"common sense" propositions which he would claim to know for
certain – and which could be used to prove the sort of philosophical
propositions which Moore was anxious to defend, *e.g.* that time is
real or that there exists an external world.

Moore's philosophic position would therefore not be touched by
justified doubts about this one or that of the propositions of the first
group. For the justification of the doubts would entail accepting
that very position. In order to prove the philosophical propositions
on the basis of "common sense" propositions all that is required is
that at any time *some* such "common sense" propositions should be
accepted as certain. Moore did not say this. He, on the contrary, was
anxious to claim that he knew for certain a number of specific things
(propositions), of which he had enumerated a great many in his
classic paper. But when in his lecture called "Certainty" which was
not published until after his death Moore was fighting the skeptic's
argument from dreaming, then – so it seems to me – he unsuccess-
fully tried to articulate thoughts which point to a more "relaxed"
relationship between the two groups of proposition. How this is to be
done in order to be successful can, I think, be seen more clearly on
the basis of Wittgenstein's comments on Moore's views.

3. So much then for certain things which Moore had said. Wittgen
stein thought Moore's rebuttal of skepticism most interesting and
original. But he would not have been the philosopher he was, had he
declared himself in agreement with Moore. On the contrary, he was
anxious to refute Moore's *explicit* philosophic position at practically
every point. Moore's claim that he knew this or that was philosophically worthless Wittgenstein thought; most of the "common
sense" things Moore said he knew are things which nobody can, in
fact, be correctly said to *know*. Moore, moreover, was mistaken in
thinking that there was *evidence* for the truth of the propositions in

question; mistaken also in that they could be used for *proving* such things as the existence of the external world; and mistaken finally in holding the allegedly proved theses to be *contingent* truths. But while disagreeing with what Moore had said, Wittgenstein was at the same time in sympathy with the tendency implicit in Moore's efforts. I think we can say that what Wittgenstein did himself was to give to this tendency a clearer and truer expression.

Let us look briefly at some of the reasons Wittgenstein gave for disagreeing with Moore.

An assurance, however sincere, that one knows something cannot by itself establish that this is so (13, 14). Moore, therefore, cannot attack the skeptics "by assuring them that *he* knows this and that. For one need not believe him. If his opponents had asserted that one could not *believe* this and that, then he could have replied: '*I* believe it'" (520). Wittgenstein is here pointing to an important conceptual difference between belief and knowledge. In order to establish that I believe that p, I need not give grounds for thinking p true. But in order to vindicate a claim to knowledge, grounds must normally be provided, *i.e.* we must be able to tell, *how* we know this. And it must be open to others to accept or to remain unconvinced by our grounds. "'I know' often means: I have the proper grounds for my statement. So if the other person is acquainted with the language-game, he would admit that I know. The other, if he is acquainted with the language-game, must be able to imagine *how* one may know something of the kind." (18.) Wittgenstein says that the situation is *often* of this kind when a claim to knowledge is being raised. Perhaps one could even say that it is always or typically of this kind, when it is open to argument whether a person knows something or not, *i.e.* when the situation is as envisaged in 13 and 14. And this is the situation which Wittgenstein opposes to the Moorean one. One could call the one "genuine" and the other "spurious" and say that in a genuine knowledge situation there must be grounds for knowing – and that where grounds are lacking the situation is "spurious."

An answer to the question "How do you know?" could be, for example, "I saw it myself," "I calculated it" or "He told me so." These are grounds on which one *can* know things and therefore types of "proper grounds" for my statement that I know. A person who is given these grounds in support of a knowledge-claim will, "if he is acquainted with the language-game," realize that they are grounds of the proper *type* – but it does not follow from this that he will accept them. He may voice doubts in the form of a rejoinder

"Did you watch it carefully?" or "Let's check your calculation" (cf. 50) or "Is he a trustworthy person?."

To answer the question "How do you know?" is not the same thing as to produce evidence for the truth of the known proposition. But when we remove doubts about the answer, we produce such evidence. If I watched something carefully, I should be able to tell that I saw this and this and . . . which, if true, should establish that it is also true what I claim to know – say that a man was stabbed in the street. To check a calculation is to check the truth of a number of statements which jointly entail that the result was what I claimed it to be. To show that a person is trustworthy, finally, is to point to a number of statements which are accepted as true and which speak in favour of the truth of what we said we knew on the basis of what he had told us.

The evidence which we produce for the truth of a proposition which we claim to know consists of propositions which we accept as true. If the question is raised, how we know these latter propositions, further grounds may be offered to show how we know them and further evidence given for the truth of the propositions thus claimed to be known. But the chain of grounds (evidence) has an end, a point beyond which no further grounds can be given. This is a thing which Wittgenstein often stressed.[6] The reason, why Moore was mistaken in thinking that his knowledge of the "common sense" truths was founded on evidence, Wittgenstein would have said, was that they were themselves such "end-points" in chains of grounds .They might serve as evidence for other propositions which somebody claimed to know. But nothing would count as evidence for them.

Consider for example the proposition that I have two hands. It would sometimes be said, I think, that it is based on the evidence of my senses.[7] But this is not, as a general statement, correct. Sometimes, however, it is correct. I have undergone an operation and been unconscious. I wake up and am not quite clear what has happened to me. Was it that one of my hands was amputated? I look and see them both. Then my knowledge that I *still* have two hands can be said to rest on "the evidence of my senses." But I did not learn that I have two hands by looking at them and counting. If under quite normal circumstances I happened to look at my hands – holding them up before my eyes – and, to my amazement, saw only one, then I should doubt *my senses* and not that I have two hands. And this shows that the implicit trust which under normal circumstances

---

[6] *Philosophische Untersuchungen*, Sects. 326, 485. Cf. also *Über Gewissheit*, Sect. 471.
[7] Cf. Moore, "Certainty," p. 243.

I have that I have two hands is *not* founded on "the evidence of my senses." (Cf. 125.)

Let it be granted that the proposition "I have two hands" entails the proposition "there are material objects." *One* way of showing that the second is *not* contingent would then be to show that the first is necessary. (For a necessary proposition can entail only other necessary propositions.) But is it not obvious that the first is contingent? For all I know I could have only one hand, or none. Perhaps I can imagine myself having more than two. And yet the truth, as known to me, of the proposition that I have two hands, is peculiar. It is not like the many truths which I have learnt from reading or by being instructed or because I have made investigations. Surely the propositions which Moore claimed are indubitable have "a peculiar logical role in the system of our empirical propositions" (136). It is this *peculiar role*, not the question as such whether we really can be said to "know" these propositions, which Wittgenstein investigates in his book.

4. The core of Wittgenstein's thoughts on these matters could perhaps be paraphrased as follows: In every situation where a claim to knowledge is being established, or a doubt settled, or an item of linguistic communication (information, order, question) understood, a bulk of propositions already stand fast, are taken for granted. They form a kind of "system." If this were not so, knowledge and doubt, judging and understanding, error and truth would not "exist," *i.e.* we should not have and handle those concepts in the way we do. "All testing, all confirmation and disconfirmation of a hypothesis takes place already within a system. And this system is not a more or less arbitrary and doubtful point of departure for all our arguments: no, it belongs to the essence of what we call an argument. The system is not so much the point of departure, as the element in which arguments have their life." (105.)

The concept of knowledge does not itself apply to that which is presupposed in its use, *i.e.* to the propositions which "stand fast" in any given knowledge-situation. This is one reason, why Moore's use of "I know" was out of place. But perhaps one could call the "common sense" things to which Moore was referring a pre-knowledge, *Vor-Wissen*. (Wittgenstein himself does not use this term.) It is better, however, to speak of *certainty* here. (511.) With the addition perhaps that it is a certainty in our *practice* of judging rather than in our *intellection* of the content of our judgments. (See below Section 8.)

Thus, for example, the truth of the proposition that the world has existed for many years past can be said to be presupposed in all so-called historical knowledge. But it is not itself an item of historical knowledge, *i.e.* it is not anything which one has come to know on the basis of investigations about the past. Through geophysical investigations we may come to know that the world has existed, say, for at least 300 billion years – or that it could not have existed for more than 500 billion years. These are possible items of genuine (scientific) knowledge. But in all the grounds which we could give for, or against, these scientific propositions it would be presupposed – though not in the form of a geophysical hypothesis – that the earth has existed for many, *i.e.* "*for a good many*," years past. (Cf. 138.)

The problem of the existence of the external world, one could say, *is* in fact solved before it *can be* raised. – In order to raise the question we must know what ("sort of thing") an external world is – or else we do not know what our question is about. But in order to acquire the notion of an external world we must first acknowledge a huge number of facts, all of which "entail" (in that Moorean sense) the existence of material objects, *i.e.* of a world external to my mind. I can inquire whether this or that object is in the external world, or is perhaps only an illusion. But whether the result in the individual case is positive or negative, the grounds for the decision will be some facts which stand fast and which entail the existence of an external world. This also explains, why there is no procedure of investigating, whether or not the external world itself exists. Its existence is, so to speak, *"the logical receptacle"* within which all investigations concerning the mind-independent existence of various objects are conducted. – "Material object" is a logical, in the *Tractatus* Wittgenstein would have said: formal, concept. (36.)

5. The propositions belonging to the system of our *Vor-Wissen* cannot be enumerated and "laid down" once and for all. Many of the items can – temporarily or permanently – be removed and treated as propositions which are supported, or contradicted, by the propositions of the bulk. "What I hold fast to is not *one* proposition but a nest of propositions," Wittgenstein says (225). (Cf. also 140–142.)

Imagine the following case: I am the victim of an accident and one of my hands is torn off. Someone comes along and finds it lying in the street. "Whose hand is that?" he cries horrified. "It is mine," I say. Then I presumably know this and have evidence for it. But when set in such circumstances, my knowledge that this is my hand seems quite irrelevant to the philosophic purposes which Moore was pursuing when he said he knew certain things. Here I could initially also have doubted what then I knew. Perhaps a hand was torn from someone else too in the disaster. When I establish that this is *my* hand and settle my doubts, if I have any, *then* part of my evidence are things "I know for certain" in that other and "deeper" sense which Moore had been thinking of.

Moore's "common sense" propositions, one could say, have the form of experiental propositions but perform the function of logical propositions or rules. (Cf. 56, 82, 308.) Their truth "is fused into the foundations of our language-game" (558) – like the truth of mathematical propositions.[8] But the fact that we can, at least for a good many of them, imagine circumstances which turn their use into a *move* (as distinct from a *rule*) of one of our language-games (622) shows that there is no hard and fast distinction between "analytic" and "synthetic," between logical necessity and contingent truth or falsehood. (Cf. 308, 319, 401.)

Moore's famous gesture, when he wanted to prove the existence of an external world, was no "proof" of a contingent conclusion from contingent premisses. It was rather an attempt to say (show) that with our *notion* of an external world we take many *truths* (*facts*) for granted. (Cf. 83, 617.) We *cannot* question these truths, since they go with the possession of the notion. Therefore it is not a contingent proposition that *there is an external world* – as it is contingent that there are, or are not, lions or unicorns. But it is a contingent fact about us, a fact of "the natural history of man," that *we have the notion* of an external world.

I should like to call attention here to two features which can be said to pervade the whole of Wittgenstein's philosophy. The one could be called, using pre-*Tractatus* terminology, the Idea of Bipolarity.[9] In the *Tractatus* this idea is reflected above all in the alliance between a proposition's having a *meaning* and it's being contingent(ly true or false). Necessary propositions are "senseless" (but not "nonsensical")[10] and therefore not strictly speaking true. They are, to use an expression which Wittgenstein employed later in his writings on the foundations of mathematics, senseless expressions "on the side of truth."[11] Epistemic attitudes such as knowing and believing apply in the first instance to contingent matters. That which cannot conceivably be doubted, cannot be known or certain

---

[8] Cf. Malcolm's *Memoir*, p. 88.

[9] See "Notes on Logic" (September 1913), printed as an Appendix to Ludwig Wittgenstein, *Notebooks 1914–1916* (Basil Blackwell, Oxford 1961).

[10] Cf. *Tractatus logico-philosophicus* 4.461 and 4.4611.

[11] *Bemerkungen über die Grundlagen der Mathematik* (Basil Blackwell, Oxford, 1956), Pt. II, Sect. 33.

either – except under some "excentric" use of the words.[12] In his writings from the years when he was working on the *Investigations*, Wittgenstein sometimes expressed himself with a certain dogmatic flavour on questions relating to this topic. It may look as though he wanted to deny, for example, that a man can know that he is in pain or is now seeing a red flash – the very things which so many other philosophers have regarded as the prototype of what *can be known*, if anything. But Wittgenstein did not wish to deny this – if by "deny" one here means that he was casting doubts on things which are regarded as certain by others. He only wanted to draw attention to "the peculiar logical role" of indubitable propositions in connexion with our epistemic attitudes. In *On Certainty* Wittgenstein can be said to extend to the whole field of epistemology things which he had before mainly been discussing in connexion with, at the one extreme, our immediate experience and, at the other extreme, the necessary truths of logic and mathematics. This extension should help us to see more clearly also the connexion and relatedness of the two extremes.

The idea of bi-polarity is related to another *Leitmotiv* which runs through all of Wittgenstein's work. This is his preoccupation with the question of the *limits of the world* (and of what can be said and what can be thought). In the preface to the *Tractatus* he said: "The book will, therefore, draw a limit to thinking, or rather – not to thinking but to the expression of thoughts; for in order to draw a limit to thinking we should have to be able to think both sides of this limit (we should therefore have to be able to think what cannot be thought)." Very much the same thing he could have said in a preface, had he ever written one, to his last writings, those published under the title *On Certainty*. Beyond everything we know or conjecture or think of as true there is a foundation of accepted truth without which there would be no such thing as knowing or conjecturing or thinking things true. But to think of the things, whereof this foundation is made, as known to us or as true is to place them among the things which stand on this very foundation, is to view the receptacle as another object *within*. This clearly cannot be done. If the foundation is what we have to accept before we say of anything that it is known or true, then it cannot itself be known or true. Moore's common sense propositions can indeed be regarded as proof that certain things can be known, *viz.* all those things which commonly are said to be known on the basis of grounds which we do not question. What Moore called "common sense" – using this phrase

---

[12] Cf. *Philosophische Untersuchungen*, Sect. 246.

in a rather queer sense[13] – is very much the same thing as that which Wittgenstein in the *Tractatus* would have referred to as "the limits of the world." Wittgenstein's high appreciation of Moore's article must partly have stemmed from the fact that he recognized in Moore's efforts a strong similarity with his own. And his criticism of Moore in *On Certainty* we could, in the language of the *Tractatus*, characterize as a criticism of an attempt to say the unsayable.

6. The bulk of propositions belonging to our *Vor-Wissen* can also be said to constitute a world-picture, *Weltbild*. This latter expression is used frequently by Wittgenstein himself. It does not mean a view of the world in the esoteric sense of a philosopher's *Weltanschauung*. It is not a private possession, but bound up with the notion of a "culture" and with the fact "that we belong to a community which is bound together by science and education" (298). One could also say that it is the common ground which we must share with other people in order to *understand* their actions and words and in order to come to an understanding with them in our judgments. It is, in fact, Moore's "common sense," *Tractatus*'s world-boundary. I know no better way to describe its nature and role than to quote Wittgenstein's own words:

94. But I did not get my picture of the world by satisfying myself of its correctness; nor do I have it because I am satisfied of its correctness. No: it is the inherited background against which I distinguish between true and false.
95. The propositions describing the world-picture might be part of a kind of mythology. And their role is like that of rules of a game; and the game can be learned purely practically, without learning any explicit rules.
96. It might be imagined that some propositions, of the form of empirical propositions, were hardened and functioned as channels for such empirical propositions as were not hardened but fluid; and that this relation altered with time, in that fluid propositions hardened, and hard ones became fluid.
97. The mythology may change back into a state of flux, the river-bed of thoughts may shift. But I distinguish between the movements of the waters of the river-bed and the shift of the bed itself; though there is not a sharp division of the one from the other.
98. But if someone were to say "So logic too is an empirical science" he would be wrong. Yet this is right: the same proposition may get treated at one time as something to test by experience, at another as a rule of testing.
99. And the bank of the river consists partly of hard rock, subject to no alteration or only to an imperceptible one, partly of sand, which now in one place now in another gets washed away, or deposited.

7. The system of propositions which constitute a world-picture not only has no fixed boundaries. It also has a very inhomogeneous

---

[13] What Moore was referring to with the phrase "common sense" is certainly not what is commonly and naturally called this. The oddity of Moore's usage is exposed and commented on in Norman Malcolm's essay "George Edward Moore" (in Malcolm, *Knowledge and Certainty*, Prentice-Hall, Englewood Cliffs, N.J., 1963).

composition. It is an agglomeration of a huge number of sub-systems, each with a fluctuating boundary and a "mixed" content. These sub-systems are related to what Wittgenstein calls language-games. One could say that every language-game has a foundation which is a fragment of the players' *Vor-Wissen*. (Cf. 560, 519.)

There is no *rigid* order among the language-games, neither logically nor from the point of view of genetic development. But there certainly is *some* order among them in both these respects. The games are of different age in the development of the individual as well as in the history of the language community ("culture"). Some could not have been learnt, until others were already mastered. Among the relatively late one's are the language-games with words like "know," "believe" or "be certain." (Cf. 538.) For this reason alone, the fragments of a world-picture which underlie the language-games from the beginning represent only a "pre-knowledge." If this is subsequently honoured by the name "knowledge," as Moore and some other philosophers have wanted to do, its conceptual character still is very different from those items to which we apply this name in the ordinary language-games with the epistemic words. Wittgenstein's "builders" cannot *say they know* these are building-stones (slabs, columns, *etc.*); yet this is nevertheless what they can *be said to know* in knowing how to play the game. (396.) Wittgenstein asks: "Does a child believe that milk exists? Or does it know that milk exists? Does a cat know that a mouse exists?" (478) and "Are we to say that the knowledge that there are physical objects comes very early or very late?" (479). Each one of these questions could be answered both Yes and No – depending upon how we understand them.

8. Considering the way language is taught and learnt, the fragments of a world-picture underlying the uses of language are not originally and strictly *propositions* at all. The *Vor-Wissen* is not propositional knowledge. But if this foundation is not propositional, what then *is* it? It is, one could say, a *praxis*. "Giving grounds, however, justifying evidence, comes to an end; – but the end is not certain propositions striking us immediately as true, *i.e.* it is not a kind of *seeing* on our part; it is our *acting*, which lies at the bottom of the language-game." (204, cf. also 110 and 229.) And Wittgenstein quotes *Faust*: "Im Anfang war die Tat." (402.)

How does it show, for example, that I do not doubt that I have a body, that this is something I, in Moore's sense, know for certain? Not in that I say *this* or reflect upon it. But in innumerable things I

say, and do, and refrain from doing. Such as complaining of head-
ache or of pain in my leg, avoiding collision with other bodies, not
putting my hand in the fire or throwing myself out of the window as
if nothing was going to hurt me. It is within this framework of certainties in my behaviour that I learn the names of the parts of my
body and of various bodily sensations and also the word "body."
Within it I acquire the notions which the various words in the language-game symbolize. But in order that my behaviour should be
describable as actions of a certain kind, it must be interpreted in
terms of the notions of the language-game itself. So, to this extent
the *praxis* at the basis of the language-game is a *pre-praxis*, one
could say, and not yet full-fledged *action*.

9. The world-picture in its "practical," pre-propositional stage could
also be called a *form of life*. "My life shews that I know or am certain
that there is a chair over there, or a door, and so on." (7.) "Now I
would like to regard this certainty, not as something akin to hastiness
or superficiality, but as a form of life." Wittgenstein says. (358.)

A world-picture, therefore, is neither true nor false. (Cf. 162, 205.)
Disputes about truth are possible only inside its frame. The presupposition then is that the disputants share the same culture or form
of life, play *the same* language-games. They must, e.g., *mean* the
same by the words they use. But sameness or difference of meaning
is possible only if there is already a certain amount of agreement
about facts. (Cf. 114, 126, 306, 456, 486, 506, 507, 523, 624.)

There are some typical cases when this presupposition breaks
down or is not fulfilled. One case is when one person denies or doubts
that which is part of the world-picture of most other persons in the
community. Then it would often be said that the person is mentally
deranged rather than that he is in error. (Cf. 71–73, 155, 156.) What
should we, for example, say of somebody who earnestly doubts that
the world has existed before he was born and manifests his doubt in
everything he does and says? Perhaps we should say that his lunacy
consists in that we cannot teach him history. (See 206.) He is not
capable of participating in all forms of our life. But we can imagine
circumstances under which we should admit that this is not really a
"mental defect," but is due to a difference in "culture." "Why should
not a king be brought up in the belief that the world began with him?
And if Moore and this king were to meet and discuss, could Moore
really prove his belief to be the right one"? (92.) Moore could perhaps
convert the king to his view, bring him to look at the world in a
different way. This would happen through a kind of *persuasion* (262)

and would not be to convince the king of error. (Cf. also 608–612.) We should then not be correcting his opinions, but combatting his *Weltbild*.

When we look back on a defeated world-picture we easily do it injustice. We regard it as "primitive" or "superstitious." We think of the change as a transition from darkness to light. This is often an unfair judgment.[14] But we must on the other hand also acknowledge that there are various *reasons* why world-pictures change in the course of history. Simplicity and symmetry are such reasons, Wittgenstein says (92). Another type of reasons, I would suggest, are diverging interests in the uses of knowledge.

10. Wittgenstein's investigations into the role of the concept of a world-picture have, I think, interesting applications to the sociology of knowledge.

In his influential and justly praised book *The Structure of Scientific Revolutions*,[15] T. S. Kuhn holds that normal science is conducted within the framework of what Kuhn calls *paradigms*. The accepted paradigms set the frame of questions for scientific inquiry and determine the range of possible answers. Partly as a result of the growth of the body of scientific knowledge, these patterns tend to "wear out," to become unsuited for their role. "Revolutions" in science consist in an overthrow of established paradigms and the acceptance of new ones. This is a good illustration to Wittgenstein's idea about the role of world-pictures. But the illustration stands in need of much more elaboration than given to it by Kuhn.[16] One line of elaboration leads us to consider the differences between the natural sciences and the sciences of man.

Even if natural science is not the uniformly growing body of knowledge which one sometimes (and traditionally) has thought, it still is, it seems, at any one time basically *one* body of paradigms. It is only during protracted periods of crisis, such as the transition from aristotelian to galilean physics during the late renaissance and the baroque, that the unity temporarily gets lost. But does this apply also to the social sciences and to the so-called *Geisteswissenschaften*? Perhaps their history is too short to allow a definitive judgment.

---

[14] In his comments on Frazer's *The Golden Bough* (published in *Synthese 17*, 1967) Wittgenstein wanted to show, how shallow and stupid the judgments made by "civilized" men about "primitive" cultures are when no account is taken of the *basic* differences in world pictures and forms of life.

[15] T. S. Kuhn, *The Structure of Scientific Revolutions* (The University of Chicago Press, 1962).

[16] There are pertinent references to Wittgenstein in Kuhn's book though not, for obvious reasons, to the late writings which we are considering here.

Kuhn seems to think[17] that the social sciences have not yet reached a stage, when paradigms have articulated with sufficient clarity to make a confrontation of paradigms possible. I am not sure, however, that he is right – and that he is not looking for the paradigms in the wrong direction, so to speak. The paradigms of social science, I would suggest, are set in the last resort by political and social *ideologies*. Sometimes ideologies try to extend their influence into the paradigmatic background of the natural sciences too. But here the effects of ideology never penetrate deep. Lenin's attack on Mach notwithstanding, there is no serious marxist alternative to relativity theory. Nor is there a respectable marxist alternative to mendelean genetics. But there *is* a bourgeois and marxist economics or sociology in their own rights, I would say. To say that they differ in valuations would not be quite correct. Valuations do not belong *within* the body of a social science, whether "bourgeois" or "marxist." This is the truth contained in Max Weber's famous postulate of *Wertfreiheit*. But types of social science may differ in paradigmatic conceptions as to what constitutes the social reality and conditions social change. These differences in paradigms may be traced back to differences in interests (valuations) and the articulation of interests to form ideologies. The fight between the interests is therefore a factor which matters to the conversion of men from the world-picture of one type of social science to that of another type, or which makes them anxious to defend the one against the other. This insight, needless to say, must not encourage us to tolerate the false. But it should make us less prone than we often are to dismiss as error that which is really a different standard for judging the truth.

---

[17] Kuhn, *op. cit.*, p. 15.

B. F. McGuinness

(*University of Oxford*)

COMMENTS ON PROFESSOR VON WRIGHT'S "WITTGENSTEIN ON CERTAINTY"

1. I am sure that everyone present will feel very indebted to Professor von Wright for a particularly lucid presentation of the main ideas of a difficult and as yet unfamiliar work of Wittgenstein's and for his interesting suggestions regarding the application and scope of those ideas. If I dwell first on some parallels (to which he has drawn attention) with Wittgenstein's earlier work, the *Tractatus*, I hope it will become apparent that this is not wholly due to my own pre-occupations but has an important bearing on the subject of our meetings.

Looking at the *Tractatus*, then, in the light of our present interest, we can see that a distinction is there drawn between, on the one hand, what is shown, namely logic, meaning, and the Form of the world, and, on the other, what can be said, namely that certain states of affairs hold, that certain facts are indeed facts, that the world has a certain content. The former realm belongs to what von Wright has called our *Vor-Wissen* and thus Wittgenstein says that it must be known to anyone who can talk or think at all. The latter realm is that in which our normal concepts of knowledge, belief, and other propositional attitudes operate. As is well-known, Wittgenstein thinks that this body of *Vor-Wissen* cannot be expressed in propositions at all. As we might say – *das Vor-Wissen ist kein Wissen*. In so far as the *Tractatus* does not merely *show* the form of the world but attempts to describe it, it stands selfcondemned as a typical work of philosophy.

A few corollaries of this view deserve mention. Even the propositions of logic are not properly said to be known. Wittgenstein does, it is true, sometimes refer to them as propositions, though often with misgivings, but in one interesting passage (*Tractatus* 5.1362) he says that "*A* knows that p" is itself a tautology when p is a tautology. It is certainly not true that everyone knows all the propositions of logic in any ordinary sense of the word "know": I believe that Wittgenstein's thought is that to know a tautology is not to know anything. A second and more questionable corollary is that the propositions of logic, like the pseudo-propositions which purport to state what can only be shown, are not properly called true. Certainly, if we had to call them either true or false, we should elect to call them true, for a reason given by Ramsey: added to other true propositions they will at any rate not yield false conclusions, whereas contradictions will or may. But it remains the case that this use of the word true is an extension of the basic use, which applies to propositions which happen to be true; and in making the extension we must be very careful not to carry over more of the notions normally connected with truth than we are strictly entitled to.

It is easy to see that a lot of this applies to the later body of ideas described to us by von Wright. The realm of *Vor-Wissen*, whatever exactly it contains, will be closely associated with the notion of meaning. Again and again in *On Certainty* Wittgenstein points out that if anyone expressed doubts about what is certain, he would raise the question whether he knew what he was saying, whether he knew what his words meant. These certainties, moreover, are not things we are properly said to know: that word has a different use and application. (I think I can take this as established in von Wright's exposition.) When we have said, as Wittgenstein suggests we must say, that these are things that must be known before I can even make a mistake, we have taken them out of the realm of knowledge proper. I have sometimes thought of saying that we could call them knowledge only by erecting a notion of intuitive knowledge, to be contrasted with ordinary or discursive knowledge and perhaps you will be able to judge later whether there is anything in this suggestion. Finally it is interesting that works of epistemology and perhaps works of philosophy in general often contain attempts to describe or outline the content of our *Vor-Wissen* and to indicate in some systematic way how our ordinary knowledge is connected with it. Now, just as Wittgenstein in his earlier work condemns such attempts as a misunderstanding of the nature of propositions, of language, and of thought, which can only show this *Vor-Wissen*, not formulate it, so his later work differs from most of what we are accustomed to regard as philosophy: it does not contain theses (such as that there is an external world or that the will is free or whatever) and the defence of those theses, but amasses facts and possibilities the consideration of which is meant to free the reader from the temptation to assert these theses or to deny them or even to consider them at all. One who does philosophy in the ordinary way can still derive much from Wittgenstein's writings but will inevitably be irritated by the author's refusal to do what I may call normal philosophy (with an allusion to the work of Kuhn's mentioned by von Wright). Perhaps some détente might be possible if Wittgenstein's recognition – I think I may call it discovery – of the special status of *Vor-Wissen* proved to be reconcilable with something like the methods of normal philosophy. Perhaps this suggestion was contained in von Wright's closing remarks: at any rate I shall return to it.

2. I have so far ignored the most surprising new element in *On Certainty*, namely that Wittgenstein there includes in our *Vor-Wissen* some things which on any other view would be contingent truths. Part of what von Wright (following Wittgenstein) has well called our *Weltbild* are a large number of certainties which are not facts or truths or true propositions to be placed alongside other facts or truths and compared with them to determine their degree of acceptability but form part of the framework within which we assess supposed facts and truths. This new element is surprising only because it is at variance with an unacknowledged and powerful prejudice in recent theories of knowledge, a prejudice from which possibly Descartes was free. Professor Williams with his rather different approach has also drawn our attention to it. It is the prejudice which consists in supposing that when we search for certainty in life, we are essentially considering a set of propositions and must first find a sub-set of those which on grounds internal to them as propositions can be seen to be certain. But once we turn away from the ‹idea that we are trying to produce a set of selfguaranteeing propositions, no one has any difficulty in seeing that we are often wrong about matters which are decideable a priori, and after the discussion of Moore and Wittgenstein that we have had I will venture to say that no one will deny that there are many certainties which neither admit of question nor belong to the realm of the a priori on any useful definition of that term.

Not of course that Wittgenstein is simply making the point that among propositions that come up for question there are those that are a priori decideable and those that are decideable only a posteriori and that among both classes there may be those that are known, those that are doubted, those that are falsely believed, and so on. This is indeed true but it is by no means the whole of the truth. There are also the certainties – that twelve twelves are one hundred and forty four, that I have two hands, that I am now standing in a lecture-room in a country foreign to me, and perhaps even that the Battle of Hastings was fought in 1066. I agree with von Wright's view, if I understand it correctly, that these are not well called propositions. In the normal way they would be uttered only in teaching arithmetic or a language or the basis of some subject or other. They are not things put forward which we acknowledge but things which all our actions in a certain area show that we take for granted. I question slightly, therefore, von Wright's remark that they have "a peculiar logical role." This seems to suggest that they are a third class of propositions alongside the a priori and the a posteriori; in reality, however (and perhaps the word role does after all indicate this) they have not an intrinsic logical character but a special relation to us, which Wittgenstein often describes in terms of the way of life, the fundamental decisions, the *faith* of a community. Now, to go back to our original point, these certainties give us the framework both of a priori and of a posteriori knowledge.

All of this is not *quite* new as far as the *Tractatus* is concerned, because Wittgenstein there points out that the *scientist* approaches nature with a framework, actually he says network, of principles which he will not *allow* to be upset. This network is not a set of a priori propositions but it shares a characteristic which Wittgenstein (wrongly, as I believe) supposed to belong to all a priori propositions, that of belonging to the *Vor-Wissen* at any rate of a certain set of men. This network fulfils the role that Kuhn in his account of the history of science assigns to a paradigm, and Wittgenstein insists, as Kuhn allows, that different paradigms, different networks are possible. In his book on the *Tractatus* Professor Stenius made the very interesting suggestion that the possibility of different frameworks held not only for science but for all our language: the world, on this view, admits of different analyses into facts and hence can be conceived as having different *forms*. Various alternative bodies of *Vor-Wissen* are possible. It is irrelevant for our present purposes that I do not believe that this is a possible exegesis of the *Tractatus*: the main point is that it certainly holds of *On Certainty*, and the question I want to ask is, what follows for Wittgenstein's own position from the fact that different bodies of *Vor-Wissen*, different sets of certainties are possible for different communities and groups? We can think of various examples, many mentioned by Wittgenstein – a Newtonian paradigm opposed to an Aristotelian one, a religious opposed to a non-religious, a magical as opposed to whatever we have now among educated people.

3. Now it by no means follows that we are not in fact certain of all the things we have discussed. We are certain of them in that they are part of our way of life. On the other hand Wittgenstein is not especially wedded to our way of life; other peoples might be just as certain of their different *Vor-Wissen*. Wittgenstein does not, as has sometimes been said, worship the common man: he simply says that no man can give up or change his *Vor-Wissen* on rational grounds: what is required is a conversion.

So his philosophy, true to its programme, "leaves everything as it is": we see that certain things are part of our *Vor-Wissen* and we also see that we can in the nature of things have no justification for their being so. But now is not his just *one* paradigm of philosophy – one paradigm among others? Wouldn't it be possible for philosophy to consist in the attempt to convert others to a different framework – or to acquire a different framework oneself? Something like this was what Descartes was doing and his work is rightly seen as a turning point in the history of philosophy, because he tried to formulate and to impose a new paradigm, which was emerging in his time. He *was* wedded to this paradigm and his reflection, which he wished others to follow, showed him more and more things which, thinking and living as he did, he could not give up. In this way he developed a paradigm which (I give here an impression, being no real historian of ideas) had important consequences for moral, religious, and intellectual life. Call it a faith, if you like, or an ideology, or even, as I have suggested, a body of intuitive knowledge. This, surely, to return to Kuhn's terminology, was a piece of extraordinary philosophy, not like either magic or science, but like the attempt to convert oneself and others from magic to science or from one scientific paradigm to a new one. The activity of normal philosophy would of course not be so revolutionary as this, but neither would it be the working out or the application of our normal paradigms, because that is our normal non-philosophic activity. It will not be a far cry from Wittgenstein, or I think from the truth, to suggest that normal philosophy is the further recommending of an established paradigm and occurs particularly in cases in which we have more than one paradigm applied to a certain area, or, in other terms, where different language-games overlap. If this is true most of Wittgenstein's own practice will not be normal philosophy at all, though it will be a valuable preparation for it (supposing the activity itself to be valuable), because his practice for the most part consists in pointing out the confusion of language-games and not in recommending which is to prevail. So it does leave things as they are, for better or for worse.

J. N. Théodoracopoulos

(*Académie d'Athènes*)

KANT ET LA CONNAISSANCE DE SOI

La voie qui même de simples phénomènes à ce que nous appelons expérience objective-scientifique ou connaissance passe par l'intellect; sans l'intellect nous n'aurions que phénomènes et sensations, nous n'aurions pas d'expérience objective, c'est à dire pas de connaissance scientifique de phénomènes. Les règles donc selon lesquelles nous ordonnons les phénomènes de telle sorte qu'ils constituent des choses objectives sont les règles de la perception et de l'intellect. Le monde de l'intellect – monde en extension perpetuelle – a deux pôles que Kant lui-même désigne au moyen de la notion de la chose en soi.

L'un de ces deux pôles est objectif, l'autre subjectif. La chose en soi est d'une part la partie intelligible mais toujours inconnue des phénomènes, d'autre part le fond intelligible mais inconnaissable des phénomènes psychiques.

La réalité foncière des objets matériels, à savoir ce que les objets matériels sont au delà de leur apparence, nous n'avons aucune possibilité de la connaître, car elle reste toujours au delà de notre connaissance. Kant soutient que nous ne sommes pas capables non plus de connaître la réalité des phénomènes psychiques, c'est à dire leur principe et leur source, à savoir l'essence de la conscience. Il en parle comme d'une chose en soi. Voilà ce que nous avons déjà appelé le pôle subjectif du monde intellectuel.

C'est là justement le point critique, formulé dans la question claire et concise: dans quelle mesure sommes nous autorisés de parler de conscience de soi et de conscience en tant que phénomènes d'une réalité inaccessible qui constitue leur fondement? Pouvons-nous appliquer à la conscience le mode de penser que nous appliquons à propos des choses matérielles? Nous connaissons tous ce que sont la conscience et la conscience de soi, malgré le fait que l'objectivation de cette connaissance n'est pas possible. La conscience révèle la présence de notre esprit. Elle n'est pas seulement la connaissance des représentations, mais elle est surtout le principe cognitif actif qui se connaît immédiatement comme présence. Kant dit que la pensée accompagne toutes nos représentations ; cela veut dire que ma propre présence rationnelle accompagne tout ce qui est perceptible, sensible, représentable, intelligible.

La pensée est le principe général de la conscience. Séparément donc de tout ce que je pense, de tout ce que je me représente, ou je sens, j'existe comme quelque chose qui n'est pas susceptible d'analyse, qui ne rentre qu'à soi-même. Ce "quelque chose" est principe rationnel, racine de la raison et des choses, puisque les choses sont objets de la conscience.

Exister signifie penser, agir selon la raison, être présent à tout état intérieur et à toute représentation du monde extérieur. Le monde empirique, matériel ou psychique, c'est à dire l'organisation et l'unification des phénomènes infinis de l'expérience intérieure ou extérieure présuppose ce principe de notre être. Tout ce qui existe doit son existence à ce principe éternel et essentiel où tout se réfère soit au moyen de sens, soit au moyen de représentations ou de jugements. Ce principe peut, au dire de Leibniz, être plus ou moins clair ; en d'autres termes il est possible qu'il y ait une conscience de soi et une affirmation de soi plus ou moins grande. Le degré de conscience de soi dépend toujours de la capacité que l'esprit a de se convertir dans son propre être. Cependant cette capacité ne fait défaut à aucun être raisonnable, soit que cet être est arrivé au degré indispensable de la connaissance de soi, soit qu'il n'est pas arrivé.

De tout ce que nous venons de dire il devient évident que la connaissance de soi constitue l'activité spontanée qui est toujours en rapport avec le monde extérieur et qui se développe et s'exprime au moyen de certains modes essentiels, à savoir la sensation, l'imagination, le jugement. En même temps la conscience de soi garde son identité parmi tous ces modes de développement et elle en fait l'unité. De cette manière l'image sensible du monde extérieur, le système des représentations fait par le moi à partir du monde extérieur et intérieur, ainsi que le système des jugements au moyen duquel le monde constitue pour l'intellect une unité, tout cela résulte de l'activité d'un fond rationnel unique, du Moi ; plus le Moi s'impose au monde et le conquiert, plus il s'avère indépendant à l'égard des objets, de la pluralité environnante, et plus il se rend compte de sa propre unité et de sa singularité. Certes, ce centre cognitif est toujours lié avec un corps animé ; néanmoins il en est manifestement distinct, comme il est distinct de la réalité psychique dont le caractère essentiel est le flux perpetuel. Alors que tout se caractérise par un changement continu et incessant, le Moi reste toujours immuable ; il reste maître de lui-même et de toutes les choses qui viennent en lui et qui partent de lui. Il conserve tout au moyen de la mémoire et de jugements et - c'est ce qui est son être vrai (ousia) - garde tout cela comme son avoir (periousia). Cet avoir est constitué de tout ce que le Moi ressent, imagine, veut et juge.

Cependant la connaissance de soi n'est pas une expression, elle n'est non plus l'expression d'un être caché derrière la conscience de soi. C'est une essence vraie, une nature pure et spontanée qui comprend et se comprend. Aussi, cette essence et cette activité propre est-elle dans tout et en même temps elle transcende tout, les choses particulières, les données qui reçoivent d'elle la lumière et l'être. Bien que donnée et dévoilée dans le temps, cette essence et cette spontanéité du Moi n'est pas causée par le temps ; elle ne doit pas son existence à l'écoulement temporel, mais elle surgit tout simplement dans le temps, et, en tant que conscience de soi, en tant qu'intelligence qui connaît les choses et qui se connaît, elle triomphe du temps.

Aristote a appelé cette connaissance de soi – qui est le but suprême de la philosophie – νόησιν νοήσεως. La conscience de soi est immatérielle, elle est à la fois sujet intelligent et objet intelligible. Plotin, lui, a appelé la conscience de soi intuition ou conversion de l'âme en elle-même. L'activité de la conscience de soi a été mise en relief, en tant que principe, par Descartes qui y a fondé toute sa pensée philosophique. Le cogito ergo sum est l'expression de l'affirmation immédiate que l'esprit se donne de sa propre existence. Aussi l'inversion de la formule est-elle toujours possible – c'est justement ce que l'existentialisme moderne a tenté de faire – et l'on pourrait ainsi dire : puisque j'existe je pense, car l'existence est déterminée par la pensée. Le fait d'être ne se rapporte qu'au fait de penser. Puisque je pense j'existe ; puisque j'ai l'autoconfirmation que je me forme dans l'esprit des idées, je conclus que j'existe. Et puisque je peux penser et juger de tout ce que nous appelons objets, j'ai la confirmation que ces objets aussi existent ; ils existent, étant donné que j'y pense, que je connais ces objets et que j'en suis le maître.

On a dit que nous n'avons connaissance que des sensations, des représentations et de nos jugements. C'est pourquoi on n'a pas le droit de dire que nous pensons, mais qu'il y a en nous quelque chose qui pense, dont nous nous n'avons pas conscience. Ce que nous connaissons ce sont les effets, les sensations, les représentations, les jugements. Cependant, cette impersonnalisation du principe de la conscience, est logiquement inadmissible, puisque penser, et, en général, juger ne peuvent pas être conçus sans cette unité personnelle et consciente d'elle-même qui pense et qui juge. En effet, je ne suis pas une machine qui pense et qui juge ; je ne suis pas un point neutre qui pense en moi-même. Je me rends personnellement compte que lorsque je pense je suis distinct de tous les autres objets et cependant dans l'acte de penser il y a à la fois la référence à moi-même et aux autres choses. Lorsque je pense, je ne suis pas au même niveau que les objets de ma pensée ; je ne suis pas un acteur automatique, mais un agent conscient. Mon existence n'égale pas la vie simple, puisque je me rends compte que j'existe. Toute autre objet se présente comme une donnée de ma conscience, seule ma conscience n'est pas une chose donnée. Ma conscience est le principe par rapport auquel les autres objects sont des données. La conscience de soi est le Premier, et bien qu'elle soit dans tout ce qui est donné, elle n'est identique à aucun objet ; elle ne s'objectivise jamais ; elle est toujours le centre d'où l'on perçoit les objets.

Kant soutient que le moi se connaît comme phénomène et non pas comme essence. Pourtant, le contenu que Kant donne au terme "phénomène," en le distinguant de la chose en soi, ne s'applique pas au Moi, à la conscience. Car la notion de "phénomène" présuppose la notion de ce par rapport à qui le phénomène s'avère tel, à savoir le centre de référence par rapport auquel quelque chose est phénomène. C'est la conscience qui est ce centre. Kant cerne la notion de conscience au moyen de deux formules, d'une formule psychologique et d'une formule logique. Par la première formule Kant soutient que, malgré le fait que nous nous rendons compte de l'unité du Moi, nous ignorons ce que le Moi est dans son essence vraie ; ce que nous connaissons c'est le mode de l'apparition de la conscience à nous mêmes, c'est à dire le mode de notre activité et de notre passivité. Cette thèse est purement psychologique : en effet, il est possible de parler du monde psychique en le considérant comme phénomène ; ce monde est phénomène par rapport au Moi

Par la formule rationnelle Kant affirme : "Je possède la conscience de moi-même dans la synthèse logique de la variété des représentations, donc dans l'unité synthétique de l'autoconscience, non pas tel que j'apparais à moi-même, ni tel que je suis en moi-même non plus ; je n'ai la conscience que du seul fait d'exister. Cette représentation est une reflexion, non pas une perception." En d'autres termes : comme autoconscience on se rend compte non pas de ce qu'on doit être, mais du seul fait qu'on est, qu'on existe. Cette autoconscience n'égale point, selon Kant, l'autoconnaissance. Cependant, la distinction kantienne est fondée sur un principe qui ne s'applique pas à l'autoconnaissance. Selon ce principe l'homme ne connaît que des phénomènes sensibles, ordonnés et objectivés par l'entendement au moyen de catégories. Pourtant ici on n'a jamais affaire à un phénomène sensible – le Moi pur n'étant jamais tel – puisque ce Moi existe toujours comme principe rationnel actif, comme acte de Logos qui, seul, est capable de se connaître. Ce mode de connaissance diffère radicalement de tout autre mode du connaître concernant les objets. L'intellect se contemple et se connaît comme source du connaître. Par conséquent, je ne suis pas seulement conscient de mon existence, mais aussi de ce que je suis, je me connais comme autoactivité cognitive, comme connaissance de moi-même.

Il est évident que ni l'expérience extérieure ni l'expérience intérieure ne m'offrent la possibilité d'affirmer ce que je suis, puisque, du point de vue logique, je suis antérieur à toutes les données. Tout m'est donné; toute donnée de l'expérience est une représentation par rapport au Moi. Kant considère le Moi ou bien comme phénomène, comme objet, ce qui n'est pas conforme à la raison, ou bien comme une notion formelle sans contenu.

L'important est d'identifier l'être avec la conscience, l'essence avec l'intellect. L'identité – absente dans la connaissance des objets – est présente dans la connaissance de soi. La formule parménidienne "c'est une et même chose être et penser" prend ici toute sa valeur.